HERITAGE INTERMEDIATE SCHOOL
MEDIA CENTER
WITHDRAWN

ORCHARD VIEW ELEMENTARY
MEDIA CENTER

MAHATMA GANDHI

MAHATMA GANDHI

Doris and Harold Faber

JULIAN MESSNER
NEW YORK

PHOTO CREDITS
Permission for photographs is gratefully acknowledged: The Bettman Archive, pp. 6, 48, 79, 83, 84, 87, 90, 91, 97, 108-109; The Consulate of India, pp. 25, 35, 56-57, 60, 61; Publications Division, Government of India, pp. 10, 75, 101.

Copyright © 1986 by Doris Faber and Harold Faber
All rights reserved including the right of reproduction in whole or in part in any form.
Published by Julian Messner, A Division of Simon & Schuster, Inc.
Simon & Schuster Building, Rockefeller Center, 1230 Avenue of the Americas, New York, New York 10020.
JULIAN MESSNER and colophon are trademarks of Simon & Schuster, Inc.
Manufactured in the United States of America.

2 3 4 5 6 7 8 9 10

Library of Congress Cataloging in Publication Data
Faber, Doris, 1924-
  Mahatma Gandhi.
  Bibliography: p.
  Includes index.
  Summary: Traces the life of the statesman who played a crucial role in India's struggle for independence from Great Britain, with emphasis on the Mahatma's early years.
  1. Gandhi, Mahatma, 1869-1948—Juvenile literature.
  2. Statesmen—India—Biography—Juvenile literature.
  3. Nationalists—India—Biography—Juvenile literature.
[1. Gandhi, Mahatma, 1869-1948. 2. Statesmen. 3. India
—Politics and government—1919-1947] I. Faber,
Harold. II. Title.
DS481.G3F33 1986   954.03′5′0924 [B] [92]   86-8734
ISBN 0-671-60176-8

Contents

Introduction 7
1 • *Young Mohan Marries* 11
2 • *To Eat Meat?* 18
3 • *A Far Adventure* 28
4 • *The Turning Point* 39
5 • *Soul Force* 47
6 • *The Mahatma Emerges* 61
7 • *Jail—and Salt* 71
8 • *London Again* 82
9 • *"Quit India!"* 93
10 • *A Tragic Victory* 103
Postscript 111

A Note on Sources 115
Suggested Further Readings 117
Index 119

Introduction

"Mahatma" is not a name, but a title meaning "Great Soul." Although the man who was given this exalted title was originally named Mohandas Gandhi, it is as Mahatma Gandhi that the world remembers him.

Since his death in 1948, his fame has continued to grow, and recently a prize-winning motion picture showed a new generation how he led the vast country of India to gain its independence. All around the globe, millions of people regard him as a saintly figure who demonstrated that violence does not triumph, in the long run, over love.

But Gandhi was also an intensely warm, unassuming, and sometimes comic human being. It is possible to know this because several of the most talented journalists of his era spent many hours with him and then put their impressions into long articles or books. Even more importantly, he himself was prevailed upon, when he was about fifty, to write his own life story.

Besides its deeply religious and philosophical chapters, Gandhi's autobiography contains many vivid scenes, especially from his early years. No matter that he is always gently teaching lessons, his disarming memories are entertaining, too.

Mahatma Gandhi

The pages that follow are solidly based on Gandhi's autobiography as well as on the writings of other people who knew him well. More details about source material will be found in the Note on Sources on page 115. One other point ought to be stressed here.

In every instance where the reader of this book is told what any person said on any occasion, the words have been taken directly from somebody's firsthand report. No trace of fiction has been allowed to intrude on the known facts about one of the most extraordinary lives in recorded history.

MAHATMA GANDHI

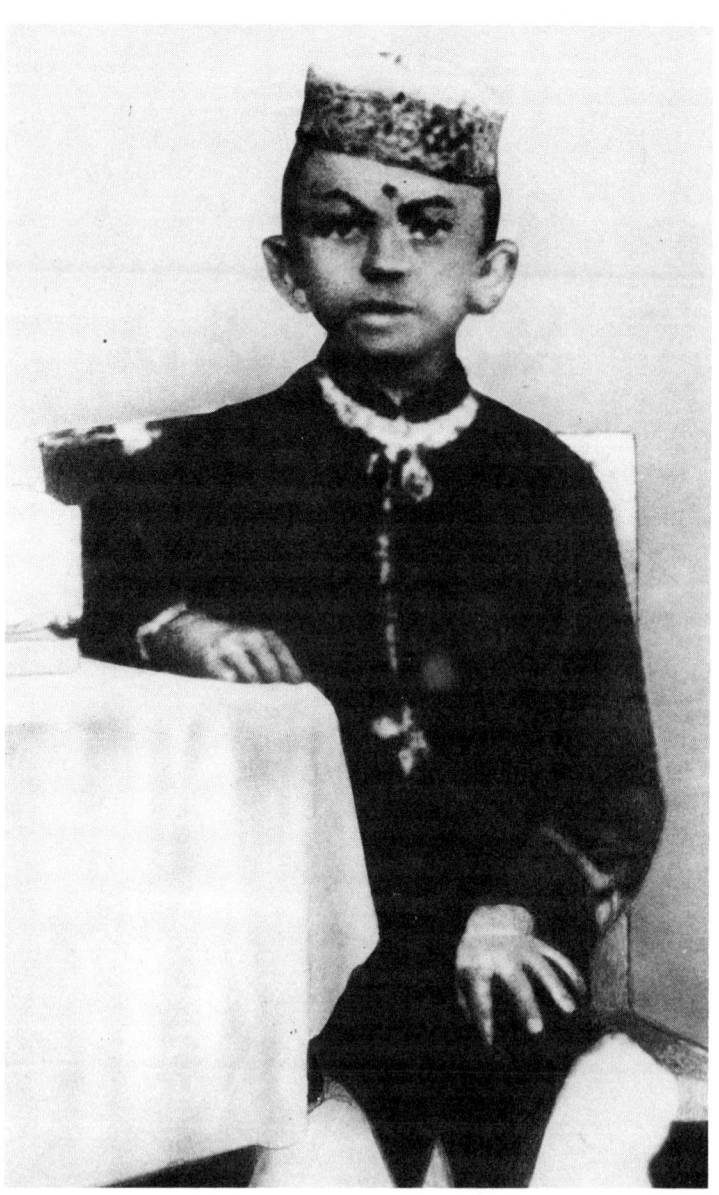

The young Mohan

Young Mohan Marries

He was quite small for his age, and looked frail. The boy's entire name—Mohandas Karamchand Gandhi—seemed much too large for such a shy, undersized child. So the nurse who watched him during his early years gave him the pet name of Mohan.

Being the youngest of his father's offspring, Mohan was especially cherished in the large Gandhi household. Although they were not a rich family, they had a good home made of limestone blocks that gleamed a bright white when the sun shone. Because of the hot climate, the house was built around an open court where relatives of every age could often be found. The boy's father, like *his* father before him, served as the chief political aide at the palace of the not very powerful prince who governed their tiny state on India's west coast.

Mohan was born on October 2, 1869, in the seaside town of Porbandar. It is not hard to find his remote birthplace on a map of India, for Porbandar sits at the outermost edge of an odd-shaped hook of land only a few hundred miles above the city of Bombay. Even so, the lives of Mohan and his family were scarcely affected by the overwhelming currents that swept across the more important areas of their enormous country.

Starting in the 1600s, adventurers from the distant sea-faring nation of Great Britain had begun setting up trading outposts at various points along India's thousands of miles of coastline. These efforts were directed by London merchants, who had organized a company to deal in spices and other valuable products from the East.

Strictly speaking, the British East India Company was a private entity, not an arm of the British government. But, as a matter of practical politics, the government became very much involved in the company's operations. Other countries in Europe, mainly Portugal and France, were also anxious to enrich themselves by controlling trade with the East. The result was a long series of raids and many bloody battles, until Britain emerged as the dominant foreign power in India toward the end of the 1700s.

During this struggle, India's own rulers were gradually stripped of much of their power. Because the huge country had, over the centuries, evolved into numerous, separate states—with a total population of more than two hundred million people, speaking nearly two hundred different languages—it lacked any unifying force that could oppose foreign encroachments successfully.

Even so, the British had to fight dozens of uprisings. Finally, in 1858, the British government in London proclaimed the conquest of India as an accomplished fact. It was decreed that India would be part of the British Empire from that date onward and would be ruled by British officials.

Young Mohan Marries

Change came slowly, though, around Porbandar. Eleven years later, when Mohan was born, local customs in this out-of-the-way area had hardly altered. As a young boy, Mohan didn't show the slightest sign of possessing any special gift that might make him a leader. What he liked best was to play quietly with a spinning top or some bright-colored balloon.

When he was obliged to start going to school at the age of seven, he went hesitantly. As soon as school was dismissed, he would run back home again. "I literally ran," he would say many years afterward, "because I could not bear to talk to anybody. I was even afraid lest anyone should poke fun at me."

Mohan had good reason for fearing he would be laughed at. On either side of his thin face, his amazingly big ears protruded in quite a comic manner. Also, Mohan thought he was a very poor student. "It was with some difficulty that I got through the multiplication tables," he would always remember.

Only in the safety of his home did Mohan feel sufficiently at ease to let his deep feelings bubble to the surface. The boy was most inspired by his mother, Putlibai. He looked up to her as a saintly person because she followed their Hindu religion rigorously. She never began a meal without praying and, whenever a holy period approached, she would take the hardest vows and keep them without flinching.

Most years, she ate just one meal a day during the four months of the rainy season, when devout Hindus observed something like the Christians' forty days of Lent. But one year she fasted completely every other day for the four months. Another year, she vowed not to have any food at all unless she saw the sun.

Then her children would stand, staring at the sky, waiting to tell their mother if they spied the faintest flicker of sunshine. Gandhi recalled long afterward:

> Everyone knows that at the height of the rainy season, the sun often does not condescend to show his face. And I remember days when, at his sudden appearance, we would rush and announce it to her. She would run out to see it with her own eyes, but by that time the fugitive sun would be gone, thus depriving her of her meal. "That does not matter," she would say cheerfully, "God did not want me to eat today." And then she would return to her round of duties.

Mohan also was impressed by another side of his mother's character. It struck him that she had a strong mind and plenty of common sense. He often accompanied her on visits to other women and on these occasions, she spoke vigorously about many subjects. Yet she had never learned to read or write—it was common then for Indian girls to grow up illiterate. Exceptional as this woman may have been, nothing about her own background was recorded by her illustrious son. All that can be said of her, therefore, is that, when she was still in her teens, her parents had arranged for her to marry an esteemed man.

Karamchand Gandhi, familiarly called Kaba, had already been married and widowed three times. Although he had several daughters from these pre-

Young Mohan Marries

vious marriages, it was Putlibai who finally gave him three sons as well as another daughter. Kaba was past forty when he wed his fourth wife. Therefore, his youngest son, the extremely sensitive Mohan, knew him only as quite an elderly man.

To Mohan, his father seemed truthful, brave, and generous, but short-tempered. The boy had no real awareness of Kaba Gandhi's career, and not until later in his own life did he appreciate how his father had risen, despite having had only a few years of education.

In previous days, the Gandhis had sold groceries—the name "Gandhi" meant "grocer" in the local Gujarati language. Like other tradesmen, they belonged to the third caste, or social class, into which the Hindu religion divided its adherents. Above the Gandhis were the priest and the warrior castes, while beneath them were manual laborers and then the so-called untouchables, who were restricted to only the dirtiest jobs. According to Hindu doctrine, an individual's faithful performance of religious duties would be rewarded by his or her being born into a higher caste in the next incarnation. Some loosening of the strict, hereditary caste system had made it possible for Mohan's grandfather to quit being a tradesman and become an advisor to the local prince. After him, Mohan's father had secured the same position.

In another matter of much importance to Mohan himself, Kaba Gandhi willingly obeyed an old Indian custom. He arranged for his son to be married—at the age of thirteen.

Mohan had just entered high school, and was showing evidence of having a keen intelligence.

Many years later, he would blame his father for adhering to what he himself had come to consider a shameful practice. "I can see no moral argument in support of such a preposterously early marriage as mine," the mature Mahatma Gandhi would write.

Yet it never occurred to him at the time to protest his father's plan. In the first place, he had been taught an unquestioning deference toward his elders. Also, the culture in which he was being raised considered the marriage of children completely acceptable, and prudent parents arranged matches for their sons or daughters at the earliest opportunity.

Part of the reason for the custom was parental concern about the continued flourishing of their family. Furthermore, the parents wanted to be sure their children made suitable marriages. Since tradition decreed that young couples did not start separate households, but remained under the same roof as the bridegroom's parents, there was no need to wait until the couple could manage on its own.

Mohan had only the faintest idea that, when he was only seven years old, his future wife had already been selected for him. Certainly, nobody consulted him about the choice of a girl his own age—Kasturbai, the daughter of a merchant. Nor did he so much as see her during the next five years.

If Mohan's father had not begun experiencing poor health, the boy's wedding might have been postponed another few years. His eldest brother was already married, and his second brother ordinarily would have been next in line. As it was, though, Kaba Gandhi decided he had best make haste and marry off both of his unwed sons.

Kaba's decision was influenced, too, by the mat-

Young Mohan Marries

ter of money. Among Hindus, marriage required great expense for elaborate clothes and ornaments and feasting. By combining the weddings of two sons, Kaba felt he could do himself proud, even though he spent less than two separate celebrations would have cost. Accordingly, he set a tremendous series of preparations in motion.

This burst of activity gave Mohan his first hint of what was in store for him. He understood that he would be getting some fine new clothing, and there would be much beating of drums and tasting of rich foods. Then, he would have a strange girl to order about in the way that Hindu husbands generally were accustomed to treat their wives. Shy as he was, the prospect seemed very pleasant to him.

On the appointed day, music rang out. Mohan sat obediently on the wedding seat with the beautifully adorned girl called Kasturbai. Then these two children stood and took the "seven steps" a Hindu bride and bridegroom take, walking together as they exchanged promises of mutual fidelity and devotion. Upon completing the ritual, they fed each other a special kind of sweet cake symbolizing future happiness.

At thirteen, they were now married irrevocably.

·2·

To Eat Meat?

*Y*oung Mohandas had been coached in his duties as a husband just before the ceremony. It was the wife of his eldest brother who told him about the physical side of marriage. To his astonishment, he soon discovered a lustful streak in his nature that made him forget everything for the next several months except his passion to be alone at night with Kasturbai.

She proved to be a quiet and mostly obedient girl. Having been taught that a wife must submit to her husband, Kasturbai did so, but she had an independent spirit that flared up from time to time. If she wanted to go to the temple or to visit friends, she simply ignored her young husband's commands that she must stay at home while he attended school.

Fortunately for both of them, in cases of such an early marriage, the wife was not required to leave her parents completely. During the first few years, a young woman would be allowed to spend six months a year with her own family. So at least half of the time, Kasturbai was obliged to obey just her mother and father, and her husband could keep his mind on his schoolwork again.

To Eat Meat?

Despite the distractions caused by his marriage, in high school Mohandas began to show evidence of having an exceptional mind. It was not that he proved himself particularly brilliant when it came to passing examinations. Although he did fairly well in most subjects, he stood out more because of the moral fervor he applied in meditating about everything he learned. At times, this intensity could even make him appear stupid. On one occasion when the district inspector was visiting his school, the teacher was especially anxious to have his boys reflect credit on him. During a spelling lesson, young Gandhi had some difficulty recalling how to spell the word "kettle," and on his slate he wrote it incorrectly.

His teacher stood above him frowning, and then with the toe of his boot he pointed toward the slate of another boy. Gandhi saw the proper spelling there, but he would not let himself comprehend that his teacher wanted him to copy the other boy's version. Later, the teacher told him he had been stupid and Gandhi smiled at him. "I never could learn the art of 'copying,' " he wrote long afterward.

Outside school, his concern with morality was even more marked. Once his father took him to see a play performed by a dramatic company, and it captured his heart. The play, called *Harischandra*, related the ordeals of an imaginary figure—an ancient king who sacrificed everything he owned in the course of one ordeal after another, because nothing was more important to him than seeking the truth. This drama haunted Mohandas to the extent that he kept repeating its scenes in his head for many months.

Why should all who were on earth not behave as

Mahatma Gandhi

nobly as the play's hero, he constantly asked himself. Because *Harischandra* made such a profound impression on him, some scholars searching decades later for the seeds of Gandhi's greatness would say it was this play that originally inspired in him the idea of truth as the supreme good to be sought by all humankind.

In any event, even at this early stage of his life, Mohandas was surely searching for some worthy goal on which to focus his ardent inner nature. Despite his mother's extremely religious example, he did not feel satisfied with what he knew of Hinduism. Indeed, he went through a period of doubt in which he rejected all religion.

Instead, he gave a lot of thought to the plight of India under British rule. By this time, there was no escaping continual reminders of the British presence, even around Porbandar. With their genius for organizing, the British had divided the country into districts where both civil and military officials supervised practically every aspect of daily life.

These British administrators came mainly from their own country's upper and upper middle classes. Not only did the Indians have to abide by laws decided upon in London, they also faced the added indignity of being looked down on as inferior creatures in most of their encounters with their rulers.

Not surprisingly, angry feelings about the British flared up often among hot-headed Indian men. Even as a young man, Gandhi did not have the sort of temperament that found release in anger. His questing mind demanded answers rather than mere acceptance, however, and when he was about fif-

To Eat Meat?

teen, he came upon a notion he took very seriously.

In the yard outside his school, he heard fellow students reciting a verse a Gujarati poet had composed:

> *Behold the mighty Englishman*
> *He rules the Indian small,*
> *Because, being a meat-eater,*
> *He is five cubits tall.*

Since Mohandas had always been smaller than many of his schoolmates, he was particularly sensitive to the fact that most Indians were shorter and less healthy-looking than most of the English. Could this truly be the result of diet? For the English gorged themselves on the flesh of animals, while many Indians followed religious rules strictly banning the eating of meat.

It is hardly possible to exaggerate the anguish Mohandas felt as he contemplated the idea of becoming a meat-eater. He knew that his parents would be horrified if they found out he was even thinking about such a step. But in this period he had finally conquered his shyness sufficiently to make a close friend at school—a sturdy fellow called Mehtab.

It didn't matter at all to Mohandas that Mehtab was a Muslim. The sometimes bitter antagonism between Hindus and Muslims struck Mohandas as foolish. He admired his new friend tremendously, because he himself still was bothered by all sorts of fears, and Mehtab boasted that he could hold a live snake in his hands. Nothing ever frightened him, he claimed.

Moreover, Mehtab excelled at manly sports like distance running and broad-jumping. Mohandas, although he had formed the habit of taking long walks for the sake of his health, was a complete incompetent as far as sports were concerned. So he listened intently when Mehtab confided that he owed his strength to eating meat.

Gandhi was aware, of course, that Muslims did not abide by a vegetarian diet. In fact, their consumption of beef was the underlying cause of much of the animosity between Hindus and Muslims because, to the Hindus, cows are sacred creatures. Thus, the Muslim slaughter of holy animals sometimes caused serious trouble.

But Mehtab amazed Mohandas by assuring him that a wave of food "reform" was affecting leading Hindus. Mehtab said that some teachers and other respected people had begun, in private, to eat meat. "You should do likewise," Mehtab advised. "Try, and see what strength it gives."

Mohandas made up his mind. He did not expect to like the taste of meat, and the thought of deceiving his parents made him tremble. Yet he felt convinced that this reform movement would in some way lead to freedom for India.

There came an evening when Mohandas met Mehtab at a lonely spot near a river, and then forced himself to chew a portion of goat's meat. It seemed as tough as leather to him, and the taste nauseated him to the extent that he could barely swallow more than a few bites.

But the worst was yet to come. After he went to sleep that night, he had a horrible dream. It seemed to him as if a live goat was bleating inside him and,

To Eat Meat?

when he awoke, he had a hard time believing that eating meat would really help India.

Still, Mohandas persevered because Mehtab said the simple repast they had sampled beside the river had not given a fair impression of what a meal containing meat might be. His friend arranged to have savory dishes made with a better quality of meat served to them privately in a restaurant. Since meals like this were expensive, Mehtab could not afford to pay for them more than once every month or two.

Yet Mohandas, who had no spending money himself, was glad the feasts could not be held more often. He suffered terribly after every one of them. Whenever he joined Mehtab for a secret meal, he found it impossible to eat any dinner at home, and his mother naturally asked why he did not seem hungry.

"I have no appetite today," Mohandas would tell her. "There is something wrong with my digestion."

Each time Mohandas spoke this way to his mother, he became increasingly aware that he was lying to her. He knew how shocked his parents would be if they learned the truth. At last, he could not stand the false position in which he was placing himself.

The meat-eating must stop, he decided. Although he still believed in the cause of food reform, it seemed to him that telling lies to one's parents was worse than failing to support the cause. Since his mother and father would never approve of eating meat, he would abstain as long as they lived. After their death, he would eat meat openly.

Mohandas felt a great sense of relief when he

communicated this decision to his friend. He was also relieved that his parents never discovered what he had been doing. As it happened, he did not ever taste meat again.

During the next several years, though, Gandhi's conduct by no means met the standards of his mature years. After he had come to cherish his wife as an equal partner in all his joys and sorrows, he would look back on this period and recall that he had frequently accused Kasturbai unjustly because he let jealousy get the better of him. At the same time, his own behavior gave her ample grounds for criticism.

Owing to the bad influence of a relative, he took up smoking—a habit that would later disgust him. Even worse, in a fit of youthful depression, he once vowed he would commit suicide. With the relative he could not bring himself to name, he walked out to the jungle in search of poison seeds. But when they found them, their courage failed.

Mohandas's deepest shame, though, involved the sin of stealing. Needing money to buy cigarettes, Mohandas began by pilfering coins from the pockets of family servants. More seriously, and yet for a more worthy cause, he stole a bit of solid gold from the bracelet of one of his brothers.

He did this because the brother had fallen into debt, and Mohandas felt compelled to pay it. The only way he could think of was to snip a piece off the golden adornment his brother kept for special occasions. After the theft was discovered, however, Mohandas was consumed by remorse.

He decided that he could not endure life unless he confessed his crime to his father. By now, Kaba

Gandhi with his brother Laxmidas, 1886

Mahatma Gandhi

Gandhi was seriously ill, and Mohandas dreaded what might happen if his father died without releasing his youngest son from the weight of this guilt.

Still, Mohandas dared not speak. After much hesitation, he wrote his confession on a slip of paper. Feeling extremely agitated, he went to the room where his father was resting on a plain wooden plank. Mohandas gave his father the note, then sat beside him to watch him read it.

Kaba Gandhi read the words his son had written, and tears trickled down his cheeks. Soon he closed his eyes as if in deep thought, then an instant later he tore the note into tiny pieces. He still had not spoken a word.

Mohandas had expected that his father would be angry and would speak harsh words and strike his forehead. Nothing of the sort happened. Having raised himself to read the note, Kaba lay down again when he had finished with it. But the tears continued. Mohandas saw those silent tears as drops of love, and he wept, too.

It seemed to him that his father was conveying a sort of sublime forgiveness, instead of reacting angrily in his more usual manner, because he had expressed the purest type of repentence. Mohandas felt his heart being cleansed and his sin being washed away while he and his father wept together. What was more, he knew just as clearly as if the words had been said aloud that his confession had made his father feel absolutely safe about him, besides increasing his affection for him beyond measure.

During the months that followed, Mohandas had sad reason to go back over this scene repeatedly in

To Eat Meat?

his thoughts. His father's health declined alarmingly. He continued to grow weaker, despite treatment by a number of physicians from different sects. Finally, an English surgeon was called in and he recommended an operation. Yet the family's most trusted Indian doctor said it would be wrong to attempt surgery on a man of such an advanced age.

Then Kaba Gandhi himself despaired of living any longer. One night he gave the signal to prepare for the last rites. Mohandas rubbed his father's legs in an effort to make him feel more comfortable. Only a few hours later, Mohandas was summoned back by a servant. By the time he arrived, it was too late. His father had died.

Mohandas was sixteen years old then. Any day his young wife would be giving birth to a baby. He would soon be a father himself.

·3·
A Far Adventure

*M*ohandas's baby son proved to be sickly, and lived just a few days. Mohandas grieved over the infant's death, but the loss of his father affected him much more. Apart from the emotional pain it caused, his father's death forced Mohandas to face some practical problems about his own future.

The expenses of Kaba Gandhi's long illness had left his household almost poor. To recoup its respected position, a family friend—a wise old man they called Joshiji—suggested that Mohandas should plan to seek the same political post Kaba had occupied.

"The times are changed," Joshiji pointed out to the three Gandhi sons, "and none of you can expect to succeed to your father's rank without having had a proper education." Mohandas was a better student than either of his brothers, so he was elected to persevere at his studies while his brothers earned what they could in the world of commerce.

Accordingly, Mohandas aimed to enter a college as soon as he had completed high school. At the age of eighteen, he passed the necessary exams, but even though he chose the nearest institution for higher learning in his part of India, he felt lost once

A Far Adventure

he arrived there. At the end of the first term, he returned home in very low spirits.

While Mohandas was on vacation, Joshiji came again to visit the Gandhi family. The old man shrewdly grasped that his friend's son was feeling discontented. Instead of berating him, though, Joshiji offered an astonishing new idea.

If Mohandas continued his present course, the old man said, it would take him four, or maybe even five years to obtain a Bachelor of Arts degree. Yet, the way things were now, the degree would qualify him to fill only a lesser political post. He would need a law degree, too, requiring another few years of study, to obtain a position like his father's.

Then Joshiji turned to Mohandas's mother. "I would far rather that you sent him to England," he said.

England!

Yes, Joshiji said, it was much easier to become a lawyer there. If the young man applied himself, he could achieve that goal in just three years. Furthermore, the journey would not be terribly costly. Expenses for the entire stay would not exceed four to five thousand rupees, a sum the family could surely raise.

Joshiji added that his own son knew several Indians currently studying or conducting business in England. "He will give notes of introduction to them, and Mohandas will have an easy time of it there."

Mohandas amazed himself. No matter that his first venture away from home had frightened him. No matter that he would have to travel thousands of miles alone into a cold country with completely different customs. Somehow the idea of sailing to England made him forget his usual fears and doubts.

Mohandas pawned his wife's wedding jewels to obtain a good part of the money he needed, and he borrowed the rest from one of his brothers. To secure the consent of his mother, he took a solemn vow that he would taste neither meat nor wine while he was gone. Then, even though he had been taught that English garments were indecent because they showed the outlines of the body, he ordered two suits of English clothing from an Indian tailor.

During these hectic months of preparation, Kasturbai was pregnant again, and she gave birth to a healthy son shortly before Mohandas's departure. How did she feel about her husband's plan? There is no way of knowing. In any event, Indian tradition dictated that it was a wife's duty to stay in the home of her husband's relatives and take care of her children, under the supervision of her mother-in-law, without complaint.

Thus, all of the arrangements for the journey went right ahead. Since no student from their area had ever done what Mohandas was about to do, his high school staged a grand send-off for him. On this occasion, he managed to conquer his shyness sufficiently to make a short speech. "I hope that some of you will follow in my footsteps," he said, "and that after you return from England, you will work for big reforms in India."

On September 4, 1888, a month before his nineteenth birthday, Mohandas boarded a ship in Bombay—bound for London.

The voyage took three weeks, and Mohandas

A Far Adventure

found it a good sign that he was spared any seasickness. Yet he felt far from easy in his mind. Although he had learned English at school, he had no experience of actually speaking the language, so his shyness kept him silent day after day.

In addition, he dared not sit down to eat with the other passengers lest he unwittingly swallow a morsel of meat. Anticipating this problem, he had brought along a supply of fruit and sweets, on which he nibbled in his cabin. At last, while he was taking exercise out on the deck, a kind-faced Englishman drew him into conversation. Where had he been having his meals?

The man laughed in a friendly way when Mohandas confessed about his hoard of Indian delicacies. That was all very well in a warm climate, the Englishman said, but it was so cold in England that nobody could possibly live there without eating meat.

Mohandas protested that he had heard it *was* possible, and he explained about his promise to his mother. That made the Englishman shake his head. In a good-natured way, he kept trying to advise Mohandas on numerous English habits. Nevertheless, Mohandas could sense that he struck this gentleman as quite a funny figure.

On the day they docked, Mohandas certainly must have caused a lot of amusement. He chose to wear the better of his two outfits—a suit of white flannel, such as he had seen English officials wearing in India. However, he noticed when he stepped ashore under a chill autumnal sky, that he was the only person sporting bright white flannels, and he felt shamed by his oddity.

Probably, though, Mohandas would have made

people smile even if he were less garishly garbed. There was something about his small stature and large ears that produced a comic impression, and this was accentuated by an element of racial prejudice. For most of the fair-skinned English considered the tan of his Indian complexion if not threatening, at least humorously inferior.

Because Mohandas was so sensitive to the reactions of everybody around him, he proceeded in the next few months to waste time and money trying to play the part of a young English gentleman. He bought a top hat and tailcoat at his first opportunity. He even enrolled in dancing classes.

Yet he found it impossible to achieve anything like rhythmic motion. Since he could not follow the piano music, what was he to do? Alas, he behaved like the foolish fellow in an old Indian fable who kept a cat to keep off the rats, and then a cow to feed the cat with milk, and then a man to take care of the cow.

For Mohandas then decided that he should learn to play the violin in order to cultivate an ear for Western music. So he invested in a violin and paid another teacher to give him instruction. Then to conquer his continuing difficulties with the English language, he sought out a third teacher for elocution lessons. This man told him to buy Bell's *Standard Elocutionist* as a textbook.

"But Mr. Bell rang the bell of alarm in my ear and I awoke," the mature Gandhi wryly explained many years later. He meant that a few sessions with the heavy text had caused him to remind himself that he was not going to spend his whole life in England. What was the use then of learning elocution? As for

A Far Adventure

the violin, he could learn to play it in India. And how could dancing make a gentleman of him? If his character made a gentleman of him, so much the better. Otherwise, he ought to just forget the ambition.

He had come to England to study law, he told himself. Therefore, he had best concentrate on this goal. But even during the worst of his floundering, Mohandas had not really forgotten why he had traveled such a distance. Indeed, he had managed remarkably well to pursue his main objective in a totally unfamiliar environment.

Besides the comic aspects of his appearance, many British people also saw something appealing about his earnest yet amiable manner, and he received offers of assistance wherever he turned. Furthermore, thanks to the letters of introduction he had carried from India, Mohandas found several friends who helpfully steered him in the right direction.

Mohandas made himself at home in a cheap, rented room where he frequently cooked his own spinach or potatoes. He also did a great deal of serious reading there. For it was no easy program that he undertook during his three years of higher education.

In addition to studying Latin and science at London University, Mohandas was accepted as a candidate for the bar by the Inner Temple, a training ground for would-be lawyers. No formal classes were held there, but a curriculum of legal topics upon which candidates would be tested provided lists of books whose contents had to be mastered.

Apart from reading these texts, the main requirement the law students had to fulfill was to attend at least six dinners a term. Naturally, Mohandas was not attracted by the prospect of eating and drinking at these feasts. As soon as his fellow students realized that he would not touch his allotment of wine—two full bottles were provided for each group of four students—Mohandas found himself in much demand as a table-mate.

Since he had no interest, either, in practicing law in England, the good fellowship these banquets fostered meant nothing to him. However, Mohandas did make some acquaintances elsewhere who led him toward private studies of immense significance to him.

By poking around the back streets of London, he had eventually discovered several good, inexpensive vegetarian restaurants. At these establishments, Mohandas encountered some reform-minded Englishmen who opened his eyes to a whole new outlook about food.

Previously, he had considered himself a meat-eater in theory, if not in actual practice. When he had given up his boyish experiments with his friend Mehtab, he had done so only because he could not bear to hurt his parents by violating their religious principle that prohibited the eating of animal flesh. As far as he knew, religion was the sole justification for following a vegetarian regime. But now he was fascinated to hear how ignorant he had been.

It elated him to learn that there was a Vegetarian Society in England, which published a weekly journal. He joined the society and subscribed to its paper. He plunged enthusiastically into the various medical and philosophical arguments in favor of

Gandhi with members of the Vegetarian Society, London 1890.

eating vegetable products, the consumption of which didn't injure any living creature.

The intense young Mr. Gandhi soon became a member of the executive committee of the Vegetarian Society. Through his efforts, a new chapter was started in the neighborhood where he lived. His shyness still kept him from speaking at any public meeting. Even so, this activity in support of diet reform gave Gandhi his first taste of working with an organized group on behalf of a cause in which he deeply believed.

The most important contribution toward his development as a leader came near the end of his second year in England. He was startled to find out that the vice president of the Vegetarian Society also had a profound interest in the Hindu religion. In fact, this English scholar had translated the Hindu holy book, called the *Bhagavad Gita*, into English, calling his version *The Song Celestial*.

By now, Gandhi was acquainted with two brothers whose interest in vegetarianism had drawn them into examining other teachings of Hinduism. They asked Mohandas if he would help them by going over *The Song Celestial* with them, pointing out any passages that differed from the original in the old Indian language of Sanskrit.

Their request embarrassed Gandhi, and he had to admit he had never read the *Gita*, let alone studied it. Yet he had learned enough Sanskrit in high school to try comparing the translation with the Sanskrit original. At the age of twenty-one, he at last began reading the most sacred volume of the religion into which he had been born.

This experience changed his entire outlook on

A Far Adventure

life. The *Bhagavad Gita* is an epic poem about the life on earth of Krishna, the human embodiment of Hinduism's supreme God. Just as Krishna in many ways resembles Jesus Christ, the *Gita* can be likened to the Bible, particularly its New Testament.

For Gandhi, the words of the *Gita* opened a prospect he had not yet glimpsed. During his schooldays, he had rejected religion because the "glitter and pomp" of Hindu temples repelled him. Perhaps because he was homesick for his own country, he approached the sacred volume with a new attitude when he began reading it in London. Whatever the reason, now it struck him as a book of priceless worth. Since he was suffering from lustful yearnings for his wife, he was particularly impressed by this verse in the second chapter:

If one
Ponders on objects of the sense, there springs
Attraction; from attraction grows desire,
Desire flames to fierce passion, passion breeds
Recklessness; then the memory—all betrayed—
Lets noble purpose go, and saps the mind,
Till purpose, mind, and man are all undone.

The meaning of many other verses eluded him and Gandhi could see that much more study would be needed before the *Gita* yielded its deepest truths to him. Nevertheless, he found great joy in recognizing that he did have a religious nature.

As busy as he was with his other studies, Gandhi still devoted many hours to reading about Hinduism and the lives of religious leaders. At his boarding house, a man who sold Christian Bibles prevailed on him to buy a copy, and he read that, too. Some of it he found rather boring, but one passage went straight to his heart.

It was these words of Jesus: "But I say unto you, that ye resist not evil: but whosoever shall smite thee on thy right cheek, turn to him the other also." Gandhi found himself attempting in his own mind to unify the Sermon on the Mount with the selfless teaching in portions of the *Gita*.

In the spring of 1891, Gandhi completed the last of the required number of terms of legal study and had to bone up for his final exams. He passed them all. Only after he received this good news did he admit to himself how much he longed to be home again.

On the tenth of June he formally became a member of the British bar. Two days later, he sailed back to India.

·4·

The Turning Point

Gandhi's homeward voyage was stormy, which proved to be an omen. The rough weather did not distress him, and he even braved the wind out on the deck because he enjoyed watching the majestic splash of the waves. But when his ship arrived in Bombay, his older brother met him at the dock with terrible news. Their dear mother, whom Gandhi was pining to see, had died. Her death had been kept from him while he was away so that he would not suffer alone in a foreign land. But now the shock demolished his new self-confidence.

During the next two years, Gandhi could not chase the gloom that had descended on him so unexpectedly. It colored every effort he made to begin practicing his profession. Wherever he turned, he saw nothing but petty politicking that exasperated him.

Instead of letting himself be comforted by his loving young wife, Gandhi often turned on her in fits of jealousy and irritation. It irked him that she was so ignorant. Yet he never seemed to find time to teach her to read and write, as he had intended.

Kasturbai bore his ill temper more or less calmly. By now, their son Harilal was nearly four, and she could see that the boy pleased his father. Gandhi took him out hiking, joked with him, and gave every sign of being a fond parent. Kasturbai could not have been unhappy when it became evident that she would soon be having another baby.

But apart from the pleasure Gandhi felt around his own and his brother's children, this period of his life was filled with discontent. While he wished to pursue his religious quest, he gained little comfort reading the *Gita* by himself. It was the custom for devout Hindus to seek a guru, or teacher, who led the way by interpreting the meaning of obscure or seemingly contradictory passages in the sacred text. Gandhi despaired of finding a guru whose teaching could satisfy him.

Furthermore, he kept failing at the urgent task of establishing himself as a lawyer. Doubts about his fitness for the profession tortured him. Then, when at last he was approached by a client a friend had referred to him, Gandhi utterly disgraced himself.

As he stood up in the Small Causes Court, his head was reeling. He had prepared his case carefully, but he forgot everything. He could not think of a single word to say; at last, he sat down again. Was the judge laughing at him? In his misery, Gandhi scribbled a note asking his client to engage another lawyer.

It seemed to Gandhi that he could never attain the post his father had once held. All he could see for himself was a meager income earned by writing routine legal documents in proper form. How long, though, could he keep on depending upon his older brother's charity?

It was because Gandhi felt such a debt to his

The Turning Point

brother that he tried to do him a favor one day. An English official was claiming that the elder Gandhi had committed some minor offense. In England, Gandhi had happened to be introduced to this man at a meeting and, despite barely knowing him, he went to the man's office and started to plead his brother's cause.

The Englishman looked annoyed. "If your brother has anything to say, let him go through the proper channels," he told Gandhi coldly.

But Gandhi persisted because he hated to disappoint his brother. "Please hear me out," he begged.

The Englishman clapped his hands and shouted an order. Suddenly, Gandhi was grabbed by the shoulders, then pushed right out of the office. This indignity seemed the last straw. Gandhi went around the town seeking help in starting a lawsuit against the official who had insulted him so painfully.

Every Indian Gandhi spoke with advised him to swallow his pride. Under the conditions prevailing in India, he would gain nothing by further antagonizing the Englishman, he was warned. In fact, he might ruin his future if he went ahead with his complaint.

It was at this low point in Gandhi's life that he received a totally unexpected offer from a Muslim business firm. These merchants had a branch office in South Africa that was engaged in a major lawsuit. Local attorneys were conducting the case, but they needed assistance. Since South Africa was another British colony, a person who had studied in England could be of real use. Would Mr. Gandhi consider going out and helping for one year?

Mahatma Gandhi

Gandhi hardly hesitated. The mere idea of seeing a new country and having new experiences somehow lifted his spirits. In addition, he would be paid enough to make it possible for him to begin repaying his brother all he owed him. A year would go by quickly, he assured Kasturbai.

Leaving his wife with two sons this time, Gandhi again boarded a ship in Bombay. Despite the unhappiness that had followed his return from England, he was no longer the raw youth who had set forth so timidly five years earlier. Now he was traveling in first-class style, as befitted a man embarking on important legal business.

It was near the end of April in 1893 when Gandhi arrived in South Africa. At the age of twenty-three, he had not yet shown any sign of having special talents or ambitions. But as he stepped ashore in the port of Durban, he was starting his remarkable career.

Gandhi was wearing a costly frock-coat, such as English gentlemen wore on important occasions, while on his head he had draped a tall Indian turban. Nearly a century later, it might seem that this costume showed only a rather dapper taste in clothing. Then and there, though, it marked Gandhi as a trouble-maker.

Gandhi did not realize this immediately. However, right on the dock, he saw Indian laborers treated very disrespectfully, and the Muslim who welcomed him—clad like an Arab, in a flowing robe—gave him a brief lesson in the facts of South African life. Indians of every rank were disparaged as "coolies," he explained, so Mr. Gandhi must get

The Turning Point

used to hearing himself described as a "coolie lawyer" working for a "coolie merchant."

But the prejudice against Indians was much deeper than mere words. Perhaps because the white settlers of South Africa were vastly outnumbered by black natives, they had come to regard brown Indians as another threat to their own dominance. During recent decades, thousands of Indian laborers had been brought to the country to work as miners or road-builders, and Indian tradesmen had come, too, hoping to set up profitable businesses. With their increasing prosperity, white prejudice against all Indians had also increased.

Gandhi's personal experience of this prejudice began the day after his arrival. Taken to visit the local courtroom, he expected no particular warmth from the attorneys he would be assisting—nobody seemed to know exactly why he had been summoned, or what purpose he might serve. What he had not anticipated, however, was outright rudeness from the magistrate.

This official kept staring at him unpleasantly. Soon he motioned for Gandhi to come forward and ordered him to remove his turban. Gandhi refused to do so. Instead, he left the room with the feeling that there was fighting in store for him. His turban seemed to him a symbol of Indian dignity. If he allowed the magistrate's order to pass unnoticed, wouldn't he be surrendering his right to be treated respectfully?

Gandhi sent a letter about the incident to the local newspapers. This aroused quite a controversy. Some readers supported him, while others criticized him bitterly as an unwelcome visitor. The publicity had one speedy effect. It convinced Gandhi's employer that the newcomer might be of more use looking after the firm's interests several hundred miles away in the inland city of Pretoria.

Therefore, a week after his arrival in South Africa, Gandhi boarded a train. By his own testimony many years later, it was this train trip that changed his entire life. The challenge it presented, and the way he reacted, also put him on the path to international fame.

Gandhi chose to purchase a first-class ticket, even though his Indian acquaintances had warned him that he might face difficulties. Because he would be riding into another province, where the prejudice against Indians was more intense, he was advised to travel less grandly. But Gandhi did not like the idea of giving in to bigotry. It was fitting that a lawyer should be looked up to, he said. Also, if the railroad sold him a first-class ticket, it was legally bound to provide first-class treatment.

The compartment in which he settled himself had no other occupant as the train left Durban. Toward nightfall, the train began climbing to cross a range of mountains, and Gandhi felt especially pleased that he had decided on riding comfortably. Around nine in the evening, the train stopped at a station. A passenger came into Gandhi's compartment and coldly regarded his fellow traveler. The man appeared disturbed by the sight of Gandhi. He left and then returned with a railroad official.

"Come along," the official said to Gandhi, "you must go to the luggage van."

"But I have a first-class ticket," Gandhi told him.

The Turning Point

"That doesn't matter," the railroad man replied. "I tell you, you must go with the luggage."

"I tell you," said Gandhi, "I was permitted to travel in this compartment at Durban, and I insist on going on in it."

"No, you won't. You must leave or I shall have to call a police constable to push you out."

"Yes, you may. I refuse to get out voluntarily."

A few minutes later Gandhi found himself being shoved out onto the platform. His luggage was thrown after him, and the train steamed away. Gandhi entered a deserted waiting room where he sat shivering—and thinking.

Should he fight for his rights? Or go back to India? Or should he ignore this indignity and go on to Pretoria? After all, he had promised to spend a year working on the law case.

Long afterward, in his own story of his life, Gandhi summed up his conclusion this way:

> It would be cowardice to run back to India without fulfilling my obligation. The hardship to which I was subjected was superficial—only a symptom of the deep disease of color prejudice. I should try, if possible, to root out the disease. . . .

Gandhi took the next available train to Pretoria. Upon arriving, he sent a long telegram to the general manager of the railroad, protesting his treatment. In addition, he called a meeting of all Indians in the area, and made the first public speech of his life.

During the ensuing year, Gandhi was extremely busy. Besides his work on the law case, he collected

Mahatma Gandhi

detailed information about the conditions Indians faced in South Africa, and he formed an association to campaign for better treatment. His efforts brought such a warm response from his fellow countrymen that, at the end of the year, he let himself be persuaded to change his personal plans.

He had already reserved a cabin on a ship bound for India, and a farewell party was arranged in his honor. At this gathering, everybody began talking about the news that a law had just been introduced to restrict Indian rights still further. If it was adopted, Indians would no longer be able to vote for any representatives in the colonial legislature.

One of the guests boldly spoke up to Gandhi. "Shall I tell you what should be done?" he asked. "You cancel your passage by this boat, stay here a month longer, and we will fight as you direct us."

A chorus of voices joined in, urging the same course. Gandhi found that he could not resist their appeal. Before he knew it, the farewell party had turned into a working committee under his leadership.

When that month ended, he delayed his departure again because so much more remained to be done. Finally, after three years had elapsed, he returned to India—temporarily. Gandhi spent just a few months in his own country, spreading the word there about the Indian struggle in South Africa. Then he brought his wife and children back to live in South Africa with him.

·5·
Soul Force

Gandhi remained in South Africa for twenty years, working for better treatment of his fellow Indians there. More than three-quarters of a century has gone by since his departure, and the racial problems of that troubled land have still not been solved. Even so, those twenty years of not very successful campaigning had a great influence on Gandhi's own life.

To start with, he was a young man who appeared to be quite fond of the trappings of worldly affluence. As his law business expanded, he bought himself expensive, English-style clothing. He settled his family in a fine house, and his wife had plenty of gold jewelry again. Yet this luxury was only part of the picture.

At the same time, he also gave an increasing amount of his seemingly boundless energy to idealistic causes. Besides his striving to protect the civil rights of the entire Indian community, he took many cases on behalf of individual Indians who could not pay him a penny. As a result, he inspired much admiration—and some hate. One night early in his South African career, he was even threatened with death.

Gandhi as a practicing attorney in South Africa in 1895. Gandhi, center, is wearing a regulation Hindu porkpie cap with conventional European clothing.

Soul Force

Two shiploads of Indian immigrants had just landed, and an angry mob of whites somehow got the idea that Gandhi was responsible for bringing the unwanted newcomers into the country. Finding him on a street near the dock, they began throwing stones and rotten eggs at him. A white woman who knew him came to his rescue.

She was the wife of Durban's police superintendent, and a brave woman herself. She went right up to Gandhi, then opened the umbrella she was carrying, even though it was not raining. Shielding Gandhi with her umbrella, she held off the mob long enough to let him take shelter in a nearby house.

Meanwhile, an Indian youth who had seen what was happening ran to the police station. Soon the superintendent himself arrived on the scene with a few of his men. By that time, the mob's mood had turned ugly again. Shouted threats about setting the house on fire made the superintendent think fast. Instead of trying to reason with the hoodlums, he decided to go along with their frenzy and began to sing:

> *Hang old Gandhi*
> *On the sour apple tree . . .*

As he was raising his voice, the men he had brought with him followed his orders. They went around to the back of the house in which Gandhi was hiding, found him, and convinced him to take off his clothing. Then, disguised in the uniform of a police constable, Gandhi escaped safely.

Most of Gandhi's daily activity was much less dramatic. He stood up in courtrooms—without his

Mahatma Gandhi

turban, to avoid causing unnecessary enmity—and he spoke softly but convincingly in defense of his clients. He composed petitions to public officials, then saw to it that hundreds of signatures added weight to his own words. He arranged mass meetings, he taught himself to make speeches in front of these large audiences. Also, he assumed the personal charge of educating his two older sons and enjoyed playing with his two younger sons who were born in South Africa.

But Gandhi found that something inside him still was not satisfied. He had never ceased the reading and studying of religious doctrines that he had started during his student days in London. Now, in South Africa, this religious quest gradually took precedence over every other interest. At last, he began evolving a faith that satisfied him.

There were elements of Hinduism that he felt a strong loyalty to, particularly its emphasis on the importance of rising above mere bodily enjoyment. Yet other Hindu teachings, such as the rigid caste system condemning millions of so-called untouchables to lives of harsh restrictions, struck him as indefensible. His distaste for this sort of cruelty made him consider, over a period of a few years, becoming a Christian.

Gandhi loved the hymn, "Lead, Kindly Light," and also the Biblical words, "Blessed are the meek." Still, much as he admired some aspects of Christianity, eventually he told his Christian friends he could not accept a religion that offered everlasting salvation only to its own believers.

In like manner, Gandhi perceived both truth and error when he read the Koran, the holy book of the

Soul Force

Muslims. The more he studied, the more convinced he became that, at least as far as he himself was concerned, there was no perfect religion anywhere on earth.

Gandhi finally compromised. Since he had been born into Hinduism, and since its sacred writings exerted an immense pull on his heart and mind, he would continue to consider himself a Hindu. Yet that would not prevent his borrowing whatever appealed to him from other religions.

It might seem, therefore, that what Gandhi decided upon was to create a new religion of his own. If he had had the sort of temperament that craved power over other people, perhaps he might have preached "Gandhi-ism" and set himself up as a new godlike figure deserving of worship. However, his concept of religion made any such grandiose idea absurd to him.

In Gandhi's eyes, religion was purely a personal matter. He sometimes said that all of his religious questing actually could be described as an effort toward self-realization. By this he meant that he was engaged in a search for a way of living that would fulfill his own innermost needs.

Thus, Gandhi's way of living began changing noticeably after he reached the first phase of his religious enlightenment during the early years of the twentieth century. He started to simplify his household arrangements and to spend more time performing concrete acts of service for the less fortunate.

Instead of relying on a lowly washerman to starch his shirt collars, Gandhi taught himself to wash and starch and iron his clothing. One day, when he found a miserable victim of leprosy outside his home, he did more than merely give the poor fellow a meal and then send him away. Gandhi took the sick man in, changed the dressings on his wounds, and tried for a few weeks to care for him in his own home.

This did not prove to be practical. But after Gandhi had taken the leper to a hospital, he began spending two hours there every morning helping to give out medicines to the patients. At this period, Gandhi was earning the equivalent in today's terms of about $25,000 a year from his legal work—a very large sum for that time and place. Nevertheless, he kept finding new sacrifices of worldly comfort that made him feel he was approaching the ideal selflessness he craved.

In 1906, a new law was passed requiring all Indians residing in South Africa to be fingerprinted and to carry identity cards. This humiliating plan inspired Gandhi to combine his religious and political strivings by creating a protest movement unlike any other the world had ever seen.

How could oppression be fought except with the use of some form of weapon? Yet resorting to violence went against Gandhi's deepest feelings. He conceived the idea of relying on nonviolent protest, of using peaceful disobedience as the means for appealing to the best instincts of the Indians' oppressors.

Gandhi reasoned that if he and his followers refused to try to hurt their enemies, these enemies would, sooner or later, find it impossible to keep on treating the Indians harshly. But, as a matter of practical politics, he did not like the negative attitude implied by describing his teaching just in terms of what it did *not* intend. Thus, the words "nonviolence" or "passive resistance" did not suit him.

Casting about for a positive way of expressing what he had in mind, he found what he wanted in his native language of Gujarati. *Satya,* in that tongue, signifies both truth and love, the qualities Gandhi believed were the highest attributes of the human soul. *Agraha* means firmness or force. Gandhi called upon his fellow Indians to use no other weapon in their struggle against injustice except *Satyagraha*—Soul Force.

During the next few years, the power of Soul Force slowly began to make itself felt. Gandhi was arrested in 1907 and sentenced to two months in prison for preaching defiance of the fingerprinting law. He welcomed the punishment, saying it would give him time to do more studying. However, after only a few days, he was deprived of this opportunity.

Gandhi's main adversary in South Africa was an unusual man himself. Jan Christian Smuts, a general of Dutch ancestry, cannily offered Gandhi a compromise. If the requirement that Indians register was modified to make it voluntary instead of compulsory, would Gandhi call off his campaign?

Some of Gandhi's friends warned him that Smuts would be compelled by his own militant supporters to go back on his word. To Gandhi, the risk was worth taking. "A Satyagrahi bids good-bye to fear," he explained. "He is, therefore, never afraid to trust the opponent. Even if the opponent plays him false twenty times, the Satyagrahi is ready to trust him the twenty-first time, for an implicit trust in human nature is the very essence of his creed."

Gandhi accepted the compromise, and he was the first Indian to register voluntarily. He believed that the strongly racist sentiment among the white population made some restrictions inevitable in the immediate future. Nevertheless, it seemed to him that removing the element of compulsion would be a step in the right direction.

When Smuts did revoke his promise about changing the law, Gandhi merely shrugged and resumed preaching peaceful disobedience. Many doubted that anything would be accomplished, but first by the dozens, then by the hundreds, Indian resisters were sentenced to brief periods in jail.

In one city, more than two thousand Muslims gathered at a temple and threw their identity cards into a huge pot filled with boiling oil. The South African correspondent of the London *Daily Mail* wrote that the scene reminded him of another famous protest against a British colonial policy—the Boston Tea Party.

But not many people sensed the revolutionary potential of Soul Force. Most of the Indians in South Africa were poor and uneducated laborers, so it seemed hardly possible that they could successfully defy a powerful government. Beyond the boundaries of South Africa, their plight was of no particular interest. Within the country, the privileged white minority ardently supported the policy of treating them almost like slaves.

Still, the stirring example set by Gandhi kept the Indian protest movement from melting away. For it

Soul Force

was during these years that this man who had appeared to be merely a mild-mannered young Indian lawyer, with certain strong feelings about right and wrong, was transformed into a spiritual and political leader beyond compare.

The process brought some painful difficulties for his own immediate family. Although his wife had gone along with being uprooted from her native land, and to please her husband had adopted many foreign customs, like wearing tight Western shoes instead of Indian sandals, the new duties he assigned Kasturbai as his transformation proceeded nearly drove her mad. Among the tasks he gave her in this period was that of waiting upon people born into the lowest rank of Hinduism, for he often invited untouchables to visit their home. One day, Kasturbai angrily refused to serve such a guest.

Gandhi raised his voice. "I will not stand this nonsense in my house," he told her.

Kasturbai shouted, "Keep your house to yourself and let me go."

Then, Gandhi grabbed her hand, dragged her to their gate, and started to push her out into the street.

With tears streaming from her eyes, Kasturbai appealed to him: "Have you no sense of shame? Where am I to go? I have no parents or relatives here to harbor me. Because I am your wife, you think I must put up with your cuffs and kicks? Behave yourself and shut the gate. Let us not be found making scenes like this!"

Gandhi, deeply sorry, closed the gate. Although their bickering did not end, from then on he attempted to consider her feelings when his own inner drives made him adopt increasingly strict rules of personal conduct.

Instead of merely keeping to a vegetarian diet, Gandhi gave up all spices and limited his meals until he ate nothing but raw fruit and nuts. He often fasted as a means of further purifying himself, or to "reach the heart" of someone who had disappointed him. He also began giving up his fine European clothing, preferring on many occasions to wear the plain cotton shirt and loose shorts of a common laborer.

Because he was becoming so closely involved with a few dozen of his followers, it struck him that they all ought to live together. He set up a kind of camp on a farm out in the country and he spent

With G. K. Gokhale in Durban.

increasing amounts of time there from around 1910 onward. Soon his wife and sons found themselves living full-time in this high-minded community.

Gandhi's four sons may have wished they did not have to abide by such exalted standards, but, apart from a bit of grumbling, they did not rebel against their father's teaching. In the atmosphere surrounding him, even lesser mortals rose above their baser instincts.

The inspiration Gandhi communicated was aptly summed up by an eminent visitor from India who spent several months in South Africa during 1912. After he returned home, Professor Gopal K. Gokhale—the leader of a growing campaign for Indian self-government—told a large meeting in Bombay: "Gandhi has in him the marvelous spiritual power to turn ordinary men around him into heroes and martyrs."

A new series of punitive laws had just been proclaimed by the government General Smuts led. Indians were required to pay a special tax, and their movements between different provinces of the country were carefully regulated. Worst of all, it was decreed that only marriage ceremonies performed by Christian ministers had any legal standing, so virtually every Indian wife was suddenly deprived of respectability.

Gandhi responded by calling a series of strikes and protest marches. Now even sheltered Indian women joined their husbands in an unprecedented wave of demonstrations that sent ripples of alarm all the way to London. Suppose this sort of civil disobedience spread to India itself!

General Smuts once more began negotiating with

Soul Force

Gandhi. To appease his own supporters, Smuts explained: "You can't put twenty thousand Indians into jail." But he had come to admire Gandhi sincerely, and the compromise he offered this time went a long way toward removing the Indian grievances. Not only was the new tax cancelled, but even more importantly, the law that invalidated Indian marriages was also repealed. Although many other restrictions remained in force, it seemed that Gandhi had won a notable victory.

Gandhi felt that he had accomplished as much as it was reasonable to expect at that point in history. During the past few years, he had begun nourishing a new aim. Now he told his followers that the time had come when he must go back to India and devote himself completely to his religious studies.

"Men say I am a saint losing myself in politics," he noted with a smile. "The fact is I am a politician trying my hardest to be a saint."

With Rabindranath Tagore at Santiniketan in 1940.

·6·
The Mahatma Emerges

*I*t must have started with Professor Gokhale's glowing report about the spiritual leader he had encountered during his visit to South Africa. Soon after Gandhi returned to his native land—in January of 1915—he went to see the country's outstanding poet, Rabindranath Tagore. A white-bearded man from a wealthy Hindu family, Tagore had recently been awarded the Nobel Prize for literature, the first such honor ever to be bestowed on any Indian. The poet took the opportunity of bestowing an honor of his own when he welcomed his guest.

"*Mahatma* Gandhi!" he greeted him.

Taken from the ancient Sanskrit, the title of "mahatma" literally means "the great soul." More broadly, it has a connotation similar to the title of "saint" to devout Christians. However, Hinduism has no procedure for formally proclaiming the emergence of a new mahatma. Certainly Tagore was speaking only from his own heart, having heard so much about this large-eared little man in beggar's garb who had such marvelously kind eyes twinkling behind his steel-rimmed spectacles.

During the next few years, a mystical process exalting Gandhi as "the Mahatma" undeniably occurred. It happened with no assistance from later-day marvels of communication, for neither radio nor television was available then. Among India's huge population, which had grown to over three hundred million, only a small minority ever read newspapers. Even so, the word somehow spread throughout teeming city slums and into the most remote villages.

Gandhi undoubtedly had much to do with this phenomenon. Not that he relished being worshiped wherever he went. "The woes of mahatmas," he wryly told an American journalist many years afterward, "are known only to mahatmas." That was as close as he ever got to complaining about the personal cost of constantly being surrounded by masses of people seeking his blessing.

But if Gandhi would have liked to have had more privacy, he surely did not shy away from assuming spiritual—and political—leadership. In both realms, he spoke out as his inner feelings prompted him, right from the moment he began to rediscover India after his twenty-year absence.

It was not by making speeches that Gandhi became a mahatma, though. The force of his selfless example was much more important, but, above all, he possessed a quality that few men in recorded history could match. Despite his far-from-imposing appearance, he had a kind of magnetism, or charisma. He communicated his essential goodness without needing words.

Politically, Gandhi still had much to learn. If he had been a lesser man, very likely he would have lost, rather than gained, influence during this period. On his way home to India, he had stopped off

The Mahatma Emerges

in England, arriving there just as the country was entering the tremendous conflict that would come to be known as the First World War. The noble sentiments he heard then from his English friends appealed deeply to his trusting nature.

No matter that in his boyhood he had felt the sting of being treated as an inferior by British officials. No matter that his South African experience had shown him how cruel colonial policies could be. Back home in India, Gandhi spoke up strongly in support of the British war effort.

He reasoned that doing so was in the best interests of India itself. Rather than aiming for total independence, he said, India should seek the same sort of partial freedom that Canada enjoyed. As a dominion of the British Empire, Canada remained subject to only limited control from London, with Canadians in charge of the day-by-day governing of their country.

But for Indians to gain dominion status, Gandhi held, they must earn it by proving their loyalty to the British in their time of trouble. Despite his intense faith in nonviolence, he actually urged young Indian men to join the British Army.

There was another reason, too, for Gandhi's temporary burst of fighting spirit. As he traveled around India—taking third-class trains now and staying among the common people—the filth and ignorance he found shocked him. It seemed to him that India *needed* the British—at least until the masses learned better habits and some form of industry was developed to end the country's grinding poverty.

When Gandhi talked this way, Professor Gokhale

fondly told him to "keep his ears open and his mouth shut." Gokhale was an old man in failing health, and he was counting on Gandhi, now approaching the age of fifty, to take over the growing campaign for self-government in another few years. Gokhale tried his best to warn Gandhi that Britain's record as the ruler of India by no means lived up to the high principles it advertised.

Fortunately, Gandhi did more during these years than make pro-British speeches. Much of his time, in fact, was spent in his pursuit of further spiritual enlightenment—his quest for Truth, as he put it.

With some of his closest aides from South Africa, he established a religious community in the western part of India, not far from the textile-manufacturing

Gandhi at a reception in Ahmedabad with his wife, 1915.

The Mahatma Emerges

city of Ahmedabad. His ashram, as the ancient Hindus called similar settlements, was a cluster of simple huts near the banks of a small river. The residents grew their own fruit and grain, and their few other needs were provided by gifts of money from devout Hindu businessmen who thought it brought them credit to have such a holy site in their vicinity.

But the Mahatma's ashram proved embarrassing, too. Besides praying and studying, and taking turns at all the menial tasks required when about thirty—and, eventually, almost three hundred—individuals lived together as a single family, Gandhi also carried out his philosophy of acting upon his beliefs instead of merely preaching high-minded principles. He took a lively interest when workers in the nearby textile mills complained about their working conditions.

Encouraged by Gandhi, the workers began a strike. All of them took a solemn pledge not to resume their jobs until the employers either met their demands or agreed to have an arbitrator settle the dispute. Under a large banyan tree on the ashram's grounds, Gandhi spoke to thousands of strikers every afternoon. He particularly urged them to avoid any violence if the mill-owners resisted their just claims. Daily, the mass meeting ended with the workers marching back to town carrying banners that said *EK TEK*, meaning KEEP THE PLEDGE.

For two weeks, the strikers' enthusiasm did not diminish. Then gradually some began returning to their looms. The mill-owners, no doubt, were greatly relieved. Gandhi, though, felt deeply disturbed by the failure of his own moral leadership. One morning he suddenly realized what he must do. "Unless the strikers rally," he said, "I will not touch any food."

This was Gandhi's first fast for a public cause. Previously, he had given up eating for the purpose of self-purification or to show that he blamed himself because some of his followers had not been able to live up to some goal he had set. Now he wanted to give thousands of people proof of his belief that he, rather than they, deserved punishment, since he had led them into making a pledge which they found impossible to keep.

By Gandhi's own logic, he was not fasting to put pressure on his friends, the mill-owners. According to his doctrine of Soul Force, the purpose of fasting was not to coerce others who might disagree with him, for that would be a form of violence. The impact of his penance however, turned out to be less complicated than his own mental processes.

All involved in the strike were so moved by Gandhi's selfless gesture that they forgot their own concerns. As the Mahatma himself put it, "The net result was that an atmosphere of goodwill was created all around." After he had fasted for three days, the employers announced they had found an arbitrator whose decision they would accept. They chose the very man Gandhi had originally proposed.

In somewhat like manner, Gandhi intervened in several other episodes of injustice throughout India. The case that attracted the most attention was that of thousands of poor tenant farmers in a remote district, far to the north in the foothills of the

The Mahatma Emerges

Himalayas, where rich Englishmen owned large tracts of land. These plantations grew indigo, a crop used to make a blue dye for textiles.

In 1917 a much cheaper chemical dye became available. The British landlords then began resorting to devious trickery, aimed at making their peasant sharecroppers pay them money for indigo that could not possibly be sold. It was an exhibition of the strong preying upon the weak. The outside world would never have known about it, if one of the peasants had not managed to make his way across India, seeking the Mahatma.

During the several months Gandhi spent with the indigo sharecroppers, he experienced British arrogance firsthand. Thus, he began to open his eyes to what could be expected when the war ended. Yet it was not until the coming of peace in 1918 that his disillusionment propelled him into an active role politically. Instead of rewarding India for having cooperated in the war effort, a new series of restrictions was decreed. The British said that the stricter rules about holding meetings and conducting local elections were aimed at averting strife between Hindus and Muslims. But Gandhi sorrowfully decided that some of his young friends were quite right. Clearly, it was the British who were doing their best to foment fears among the seventy million Muslims that, in a free India, they would be persecuted unbearably by the country's two hundred million Hindus. In addition, other smaller religious communities, such as the Sikhs and Parsees, were being given special benefits as a means of insuring their loyalty to the British.

Once Gandhi became convinced of all this, he

Mahatma Gandhi

cast about for a dramatic way to prove that Indians of the two major religions, as well as the members of many smaller sects, could live together peacefully. One morning in the spring of 1919, shortly after the humiliating new laws took effect, he awoke with a joyous feeling. He was visiting the city of Madras to attend a meeting of a political action committee.

"Last night," he told the people at the meeting a few hours later, "the idea came to me in a dream that we should call on the country to observe a general *hartal.*"

The word *hartal*, combining two Hindi words meaning "shop" and "lock," meant a complete halt in every sort of business. Gandhi explained that what he had in mind was a brief stoppage all over the country—not a strike, but a few days of prayer and fasting to demonstrate how strongly Indians of every religion wished to be free. It was extremely important, he added, that the *hartal* be observed without even one brick being thrown. The whole point of the demonstration was to display discipline as well as determination.

Gandhi's colleagues on the committee applauded his idea with great vigor. While the religious aspect of the plan had tremendous appeal in a country like India, some who thought of themselves as less spiritual but more practical than the Mahatma liked his idea for another reason. There was no way that millions of mostly poor and uneducated Indians could defeat the mighty British by force of arms. If the Indians were to win, they would have to win by appealing to the best instincts of their oppressors.

The plan for a nationwide *hartal* was adopted, and it was an amazing success. Early in April of

The Mahatma Emerges

1919, the British were stunned by the stoppage of trains, the closing of shops, the total shutdown of economic life everywhere in the vast subcontinent they ruled.

But the work stoppage was not entirely peaceful. In several cities fires were started, telegraph wires were cut, and some English officials were beaten up. When reports of these incidents reached Gandhi, he was heartsick. Then, thinking back to South Africa, he recalled that only a few thousand protesters had taken part in his campaign there. And he had succeeded in reaching them with his message of nonviolence.

Here, millions had joined the campaign. Wasn't it his own fault that he had given the signal for such a massive demonstration without making sure the importance of avoiding violence was understood? Gandhi announced that he had made "a Himalayan miscalculation."

All resistance against the British must cease, the Mahatma said. Not until the people of India were ready to accept blows without hitting back, to rise above the terrible idea of vengeance, could a campaign based on Soul Force hope to succeed.

Yet even the Mahatma could not cool the passions that had been aroused. During the next several weeks, there were riots in many parts of India. The British felt threatened by a full-scale revolt. After generations of being the unchallenged conquerors of this enormous Asian land, most of the British hierarchy could not help feeling furious and many were frightened.

A peaceful Indian protest in the holy city of Amritsar provoked a fierce reaction from the British commander there. When he heard that a few thousand men, women, and children had gathered at an open-air meeting, General Reginald Dyer rushed to the scene with several dozen armed men. It turned out that the crowd was in an area surrounded by a high brick wall. There was no escape except through one narrow passageway, where the general planted himself with his squad of riflemen. Then Dyer commanded his men to fire, and to keep firing until their ammunition ran out.

Before the shooting ceased, 379 Indians had been killed in cold blood and 1,137 wounded. These precise figures were provided during a formal inquiry the British held to investigate the facts about "the Amritsar Massacre," as newspapers in many countries described the slaughter. The British retained a basic sense of decency, and public opinion back home in Britain had demanded the truth about the matter.

Yet the temper of British officials in India had been so tried by Indian threats to their own privilege that they reacted quite differently. To them, General Dyer was a hero, and when London ordered his retirement, his old comrades all over India contributed out of their own pockets to reward him with a handsome pension.

After the wave of Indian rioting following Amritsar finally subsided, the head of the British government in India took a step he had not dared to take at the height of the trouble. The British Viceroy, in the spring of 1922, signed a warrant ordering the arrest of Mahatma Gandhi.

·7·
Jail—and Salt

*I*t was one of the most unusual trials ever held. One hot day in March 1922, in Ahmedabad, near Gandhi's ashram, hundreds of his followers—and a few foreign journalists—jammed into the British court. Then the British prosecutor for the area rose to state the case against the accused.

The charge, he said, was of exciting "disaffection" toward the lawful British government in India. This had been done specifically by writing three articles published in the magazine *Young India*, though it could be proved, if need be, that the defendant had begun preaching disaffection long before the publication of the said three articles.

Gandhi himself broke in at this point. "I plead guilty to all the charges," he said gently.

Nevertheless, the judge allowed the prosecutor to continue describing Gandhi's campaign of "noncooperation" over the past several years. Clearly, the aim of such defiance was to undermine the government's authority. In this campaign, it was true that the accused preached nonviolence, the prosecutor admitted, but, inasmuch as some of his supporters had undoubtedly committed violent acts, what difference did that make?

The judge then addressed the defendant. "Mr. Gandhi," he said, "do you wish to make a statement on the question of sentence?"

Gandhi said he did. After pausing to unfold and put on his spectacles, he proceeded to read one of the most extraordinary declarations any prisoner anywhere had ever made. With simple eloquence, he traced his whole career:

"My public life began in 1893 in South Africa in troubled weather. My first contact with British authority in that country was not of a happy character. I discovered that as a man and as an Indian I had no rights. More correctly, I discovered that I had no rights as a man because I was an Indian.

"But I was baffled. . . ." Then he briefly recounted his experiences over nearly thirty years of attempting, by nonviolent means, to win fair treatment for his fellow Indians, to secure for them the same rights that the high principles of British law guaranteed British citizens everywhere. It was only because of the way Indians were mistreated under Britain's rule of their own country, Gandhi said, that he himself had come to deem it a sin to have affection for the British system.

"I believe," he said, "that I have rendered a service to India and England by showing in noncooperation the way out of the unnatural state in which both are now living. In my humble opinion, noncooperation with evil is as much a duty as is cooperation with good."

So promoting disaffection was exactly what he had been doing, Gandhi admitted. "I am here, therefore," he said, "to invite and submit cheerfully to the highest penalty that can be inflicted on me for

Jail — and Salt

what in law is a deliberate crime and what appears to me to be the highest duty of a citizen." He concluded with a remarkable challenge to the judge:

> The only course open to you, the judge, is either to resign your post and thus dissociate yourself from evil, if you feel that the law you are called upon to administer is an evil and that in reality I am innocent; or to inflict on me the severest penalty, if you believe that the system and the law you are assisting to administer are good for the people of this country, and that my activity is therefore injurious to the public weal.

Gandhi's words appeared to impress the judge deeply. Still, he said it was *his* duty to sentence the accused to six years in jail. "I should like to say," Judge Broomsfield added, "that if the course of events in India makes it possible for the government to reduce the period and release you, no one will be better pleased than I."

As soon as the judge left the room, the Indian spectators crowded around the Mahatma. There was much sobbing by both men and women. But Gandhi remained smiling and cool, giving encouragement to his weeping admirers. After they were persuaded to depart, Gandhi calmly went with a pair of deputies, who escorted him to the regional prison.

In South Africa, Gandhi had been jailed a few times, and those short stays behind bars had profoundly influenced him. Instead of bemoaning his captivity, he had felt uplifted by a mystic kinship with his unfortunate cellmates. "The real road to happiness," he had written, "lies in going to jail and undergoing suffering and privations there in the interest of one's country and religion."

It was during one of these prison terms that Gandhi had decided never again to dress in European style, for the plain garb of a prisoner gave him a wonderful sense of freedom from material desires. In a South African jail, he had also made the acquaintance of a writer from the distant United States, through the magic of the printed word. Henry David Thoreau's essay entitled "Civil Disobedience" had deeply affected Gandhi's own thinking.

The New Englander Thoreau, shortly before the Civil War, had refused to pay taxes levied by a government that condoned Negro slavery. "The only obligation which I have the right to assume is to do at any time what I think right," he had written. Of his experience in a Massachusetts jail, Thoreau noted: "I did not feel for a moment confined, and the walls seemed a great waste of stone and mortar." Halfway around the world, Gandhi had copied down these passages and he never forgot them.

He used the enforced leisure to which he had been sentenced as a period for strengthening his own spiritual convictions. He was allowed to read and write, and he finally found time to start a project some of his friends had often urged upon him—the writing of his own story of his early life. But after twenty-two months in jail, Gandhi began to feel very ill.

Taken by ambulance to a British hospital, Gandhi had an emergency operation to remove an acutely

Jail — and Salt

inflamed appendix. Despite the Mahatma's firm ideas favoring only the simplest medical treatment, he profusely thanked the surgeon who saved his life. Even though the surgery was successful, Gandhi's recovery was slow. Because of his weakness, and also because protests against the government had gradually waned during his imprisonment, the British decided it would be wise to pardon him, instead of returning him to jail. Thus, in February of 1924, Gandhi arrived back at his ashram.

The court order that set him free had placed no limits on his future activities. Yet Gandhi appeared to feel bound not to stir any major controversy during the remainder of the period he might have been kept in prison. While he was far from idle, the

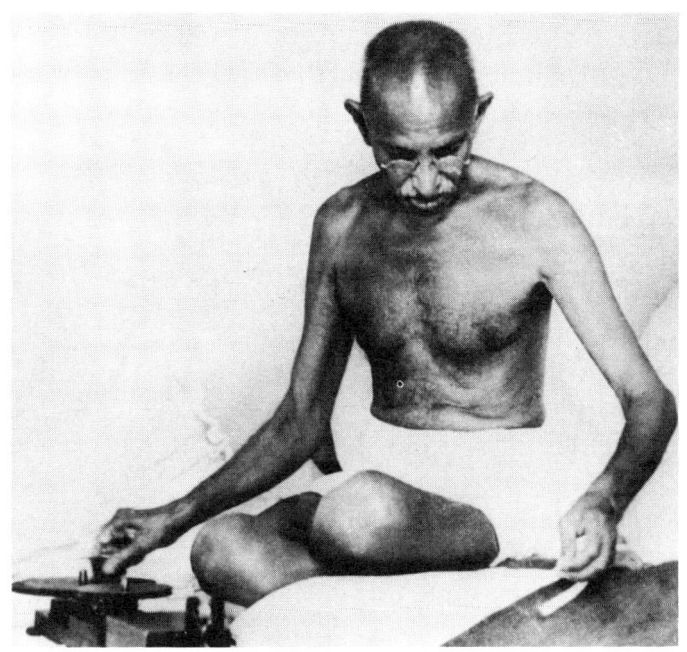

Gandhi spinning

Mahatma Gandhi

Mahatma spent the next four years mainly out of the public eye, traveling from village to village as a teacher rather than a political leader.

Only an idealist like Gandhi could have seriously expected to cure his country's terrible poverty with spinning wheels. But it seemed to him that many of India's economic problems could be solved if the country simply turned its back on modern mass production. Gandhi had taken up spinning himself, and he tried to encourage millions of men and women to follow his example.

In the old days, the Mahatma kept telling rural villagers, every family had kept its spinning wheel whirring in the intervals between planting and harvesting its own food. This cottage industry had not only provided homespun cloth for the family's own garments, but also brought in money to purchase food in years of crop failure. Thus, there were no famines, and even the poorest peasants earned enough to live decently.

Furthermore, Gandhi claimed that a revival of rural spinning could serve an important political purpose. If India stopped buying cloth exported by English textile mills, wouldn't the British find that holding onto India was no longer profitable? In fact, the boycott of British textiles that he advocated did have some impact, for it became a badge of honor for Indians to wear only homespun cotton clothing. But, in the long run, this campaign's most notable achievement was to make the spinning wheel itself the symbol of Indian independence.

During these years, the Mahatma also used his own vast prestige to teach lessons in religious tolerance. Trouble flared up between Hindus and Mus-

Jail—and Salt

lims late in 1924, and Gandhi chose a unique means of communicating his disappointment. Everybody knew that the Mahatma had been born a Hindu. It therefore stirred a great surge of emotion when he announced that he was going to fast for twenty-one days, staying at the home of a Muslim friend, with two Muslim physicians watching over him.

Gandhi trusted that his personal sacrifice, under these circumstances, would bring a similar spirit of brotherhood all over the country. Certainly Indians of every religion felt an immense relief when the twenty-one days ended, and a weak but smiling Mahatma drank some orange juice. However, even if no new fighting erupted, in several crowded cities it still seemed that dissension was simmering not far below the surface.

Among the Hindu majority, Gandhi continued to oppose the special intolerance Hinduism fostered against its millions of untouchables. To reduce their stigma, he decided on a new name for the members of this downtrodden group. He called them *Harijans*, which means "Children of God," and he also gave that title to a magazine he sponsored.

Since he never hesitated to associate with anyone born into this lowest caste, even drinking the water from wells reserved only for untouchables, Gandhi was sometimes treated like an untouchable by high-caste orthodox Hindus. He was roughly ordered away when it appeared that merely his shadow might contaminate them. Much more frequently, though, his own aura of almost godlike holiness protected him from any insults.

Whether at his own ashram or during his travels, the Mahatma was often surrounded by hordes of people straining to see him, to touch him, to ask his blessing. Sometimes his sandaled feet and bare legs were covered with scratches caused by men, women, and children who pressed too close. While Gandhi could not avoid becoming an object of worship, he did his best to discourage what he called "this type of idolatry."

It was a form of superstition, he said, and India must rise above such ignorance if the country were ever to deserve freedom. Actually, all of his teaching during this relatively serene period revolved around the same basic theme of preparing for eventual independence.

In 1928, a new wave of unrest brought the issue forward again, just as Gandhi's self-imposed term of political inactivity was ending. Without his calming influence, some hot-headed young nationalists had begun pressing for an immediate step, something like the American Declaration of Independence. It did not seem to worry them that, by making such a proclamation, they would be implying that they, too, were willing to fight a revolutionary war.

Gandhi could not accept this idea. Instead, he sought an opportunity for some kind of negotiation with the British that might lead to an offer of dominion status. During 1929, there were signs in London and in the Indian capital of New Delhi that this effort might succeed. It failed, however. Then the Mahatma stood by in silence while the All-India Congress, which was the main organization working for the country's freedom, adopted a resolution demanding independence within the coming year.

At times, Gandhi had presided over the Congress, but more often he served just as its unofficial

Mahatma Gandhi with the "Army of Crusaders" on their way to break the British Salt monopoly laws.

inspiration. Now he held no title, although everybody knew he was the soul of the movement. The poet Tagore, more outspoken than most Indians, had the boldness to ask the Mahatma early in 1930 what in the world he was going to recommend to carry out the resolve of the Congress.

"I am furiously thinking day and night," Gandhi told him, "and I do not see any light coming out of the surrounding darkness."

He kept remembering the phrase "civil disobedience" that he had learned from his reading of the American Thoreau. By the beginning of March, Gandhi had thought of exactly the sort of civil disobedience campaign he had been seeking. It would be easy to explain to the great mass of uneducated Indians, yet it was bound to advance the cause of Indian independence.

Mahatma Gandhi

What Gandhi had in mind was to create a major issue—over ordinary salt.

One of the features of British rule of the country was a law declaring the manufacture of common salt to be a British monopoly. No matter that India had thousands of miles of coastline lapped by salty waves, no Indian was allowed to extract salt from the water. Only British-owned salt works could do this, and the British monopoly deprived many Indians of an easy opportunity to make money.

To call attention to this injustice—and to challenge it—on March 12, 1930, Mahatma Gandhi set out on foot from his ashram, accompanied by seventy-eight men and women who lived there with him.

The aim of his Salt March was to walk all the way to the seacoast, a distance of about two hundred miles. Upon arriving at the water's edge, Gandhi promised, he and his small band of pilgrims would defy the mighty British Empire simply and peaceably, by filling a few pans with salty foam and then letting them sit in the sun until all the liquid evaporated, leaving handfuls of pure salt.

To start with, hardly anybody besides Gandhi expected such a simple sort of demonstration to accomplish much. But like some ancient myth about a contest between good and evil, like the Bible story of David and Goliath, the idea captured the imagination of a few foreign journalists. They hired cars and came to see what might happen.

In the stifling heat of India's dry season, the marchers advanced slowly along winding dirt roads shaded only by an occasional tree. At the age of sixty, the Mahatma made light of the hardship

Jail—and Salt

involved. "Less than ten miles a day—without much luggage," he said. "Child's play!"

His cheerful words were telegraphed to newspapers as far away as Chicago. Day by day, more reporters kept arriving along the line of march. Something amazing seemed to be occurring.

In every remote village the procession reached, it was welcomed with festive banners and bouquets of flowers. Scores of peasants kept joining the original small band until twenty-four days later, on the evening of April 5, there were thousands of people prayerfully watching as the Mahatma bent down at the water's edge, near a little town called Dandi, and filled a pan to its rim.

This ceremony ending Gandhi's Salt March became a front-page story all over the world.

· 8 ·

London Again

At first, the British tried to ignore Gandhi's handful of salt. Wasn't the gesture rather like a tiny insect buzzing around a lion's tail? What a joker the little man was turning into, one Englishman would tell another. But soon they stopped laughing.

As if some magical signal had been sounded, up and down both the east and the west coasts of India tens of thousands of people started making their own salt. Illegal salt was openly sold on the streets of the country's major cities. The top British officials kept murmuring it was better not to risk causing any riots over such a silly issue. In a month or so the salt craze would surely stop by itself.

Instead, this sudden surge of defiance spawned other kinds of protest. Shops that sold British textiles or any product made in Britain began to find their entrances blocked by a picket line of Indian men and women holding hand-lettered banners. "DON'T BUY BRITISH!" the signs proclaimed. Such interference with commerce spurred the British authorities into action.

Squads of police brandishing a particularly ugly kind of steel-tipped club known as a *lathi* pounced on the pickets and herded them off to jail. But no

London Again

sooner had one group been arrested than another appeared. All over India, mass arrests were filling every available cell—and still more pickets kept arriving outside British-owned shops.

A month after the Salt March had ended, the British Viceroy decided that enough was enough. It was time to prove that the tail of the British lion could not be tweaked indefinitely. He signed an order calling for the arrest of the undoubted inspirer of this virtual mutiny.

Around midnight on May 4, 1930, a local police superintendent found the Mahatma sleeping under a mango tree near Dandi, where the marchers remained camped. Within a few hours, Gandhi was in prison again.

No trial was held this time. To avoid giving Gandhi another opportunity to speak up about the unfairness of British justice, the most basic princi-

Indian women picket foreign cloth shops and boycott British goods.

Mahatma Gandhi

ple of British common law was violated. Without any chance to hear the charge against him, or to defend himself, the leader of almost four hundred million Indians was unceremoniously clapped behind bars.

Yet even this absence of ceremony served Gandhi's purpose. By treating him so harshly, the British merely increased sympathy for his cause among freedom-loving people in other countries. In India itself, the arrest triggered an unprecedented wave of nonviolent revolt.

Gandhi thought his long years of teaching had finally made his fellow countrymen realize that they must rely on Soul Force, rather than violence, to gain self-government. Events immediately following his imprisonment justified his faith.

Indian mounted policeman disperses salt raiders at Bombay.

London Again

Three weeks later, a group of 2,500 volunteers decided to practice civil disobedience by peacefully attempting to enter a government salt works north of Bombay. The property was guarded by police, who had been warned of impending trouble. An American journalist, Webb Miller of the United Press, had also been alerted.

Miller stood watching incredulously as a long column of Indian demonstrators approached the factory gate. The police began whacking heads with their steel-tipped *lathis*. One Indian after another fell down, writhing in pain. Miller wrote:

> Not one of the marchers even raised an arm to fend off the blows. They went down like tenpins. From where I stood I heard the sickening whack of the clubs on unprotected skulls. The waiting crowd of marchers groaned and sucked in their breath in sympathetic pain at every blow. . . . The survivors, without breaking ranks, silently and doggedly marched on until struck down.
>
> They marched steadily, with heads up, without the encouragement of music or cheering or any possibility that they might escape serious injury or death. . . .

Since the news service that Miller worked for had subscribers in many countries, his story was printed in more than a thousand newspapers. It brought widespread outrage, even in England. It was probably the crucial factor that led the British government to decide, after all, that it had better start negotiating with Mahatma Gandhi.

The poet Tagore thought that, at least unofficially, Britain had already lost India. The only valid claim the British could make to justify holding onto their largest colony was the high-minded argument that they were a civilizing influence on a backward land, Tagore declared. But how could that argument survive the revelation of the terrible beatings outside the salt works? He insisted Britain's policy was based on nothing more noble than the idea of "Western race supremacy."

British pride in their far-flung empire kept the leaders of the government in London from authorizing any quick action. It took several months until Gandhi was even released from prison, but he did not mind the delay. "I have been quite happy and making up for arrears in sleep," he wrote to one of his closest aides. Finally, early in January of 1931, he was let go; a month later, a historic process began.

At the Viceroy's palace in Delhi, Gandhi began a series of preliminary talks that were unlike any previous meeting between an Indian and the head of the British government in India. Instead of being treated as a humble petitioner, the Mahatma was accorded the sort of diplomatic courtesy the leader of a recognized nation would expect to receive. Wearing only a white cotton loincloth and a pair of homemade wooden sandals, Gandhi walked up the wide front steps of the palace into a gorgeously decorated meeting hall. Ornately uniformed sentries stood at attention. Coming straight from jail, Gandhi was quite amused by the contrast.

But the spectacle infuriated another great man. In London, Winston Churchill made a speech protesting what was occurring in New Delhi. Already a noted leader of Britain's Conservative party—al-

London Again

though it would be another ten years before he became one of the most outstanding British prime ministers—Churchill spoke with his customary elo-

Mahatma Gandhi arriving in Folkstone to attend the Round Table Conference in London, 1931.

quence on behalf of maintaining his country's imperial grandeur.

He was appalled, Churchill said, by the "nauseating and humiliating spectacle of this one-time Inner Temple lawyer, now seditious fakir [a religious beggar], striding half-naked up the steps of the Viceroy's palace, there to negotiate and parley on equal terms with the representative of the King-Emperor." (Britain's King George V also held the title of Emperor of India.)

But a worse sight, from Churchill's aristocratic point of view, followed the series of preliminary discussions in Delhi. On September 12, 1931, Mahatma Gandhi arrived in London to take part in what was termed a round table conference on the future status of India.

Accompanied by his youngest son and a few other aides, Gandhi spent eleven astonishing weeks visiting England. Officially, he was representing the All-India Congress which, under the talented guidance of a young lawyer named Jawaharlal Nehru, had become a highly organized political party with branches throughout the country. Instead of sending a large delegation to London, however, Nehru relied solely on the Mahatma. In their own land and elsewhere, it had become obvious that Gandhi was the voice of India.

In London, he was also the object of great curiosity. Whether Gandhi liked it or not, he had to realize that he had become internationally famous. Even the King of England wanted to meet him, and he was invited for tea at Buckingham Palace.

British newspapers raised a big fuss over what Gandhi would wear on this formal occasion. Be-

London Again

cause the autumn climate of England could be quite chilly, as he well remembered from his student days, he had brought along a heavy cotton shawl to wrap around his shoulders, along with his usual loincloth and sandals. Gandhi did not even think of adding to this costume when he went to take tea with King George and Queen Mary. But as he was leaving Buckingham Palace, a reporter shouted out a question.

Had he worn enough clothing on this important occasion?

Gandhi smiled amiably. "The King had enough on for both of us," he said.

By his unassuming good humor under the searchlight of so much publicity, Gandhi won respect even among die-hard Tories, as some of Britain's Conservatives were often called. Among the ordinary people, who were more likely to vote for the Labour party, he made quite a hit. They liked the idea that he stayed at an unpretentious lodging in a slum area of London, instead of at a fancy hotel, and that when he went out on his daily walks, he spoke cheerfully to the passers-by who smiled at him.

One brash youngster gaped at him and then demanded, "Hey, Gandhi, where's your trousers?" The Mahatma laughed delightedly.

Yet he did his best to make his visit serve a more serious purpose than merely amusing the British public. He made uncounted speeches at public meetings, he held private conversations with important people, he even journeyed to the textile manufacturing area in the north of England to assure the workers there that the Indian boycott of British goods—which had caused quite a bit of

Mahatma Gandhi

Mahatma Gandhi with cheering mill workers in Lancashire, England.

unemployment—was an unavoidable by-product of India's quest for freedom. His bravery disarmed critics who might otherwise have booed him. At a meeting of textile workers that he addressed, a man stood up and said, "I am one of the unemployed, but if I was in India, I would say the same thing Mr. Gandhi is saying."

It was this sort of hands-across-the-sea activity that struck Gandhi as the real purpose of his visit. He tirelessly went wherever he was invited, seeking sympathy for the Indian cause. A diary kept by one of his aides showed that on an average day during those eleven weeks, he went to bed at two in the morning, woke an hour and half later for prayers and writing letters, rested from five to six, and then carried on uninterruptedly until one the next morning.

London Again

As a result, the Mahatma occasionally dozed during sessions of the round table conference. It did not matter much. It turned out that the British did not really want to negotiate any agreement granting freedom to India. The pride and prejudice of respected Conservatives like Winston Churchill had effectively dampened any impulse toward granting Indian demands.

The British negotiators adopted a policy that Gandhi thought was like putting the cart before the horse. They insisted that dozens of specific details must be settled before they could make any offer of dominion status. The main stumbling block they kept bringing up had to do with the large Muslim minority in India. Saying they had to make sure the

Gandhi attends Round Table Conference in London at St. James Palace, September 1931.

Muslims would never be oppressed by the Hindu majority, they proposed arrangements Gandhi considered dangerously mistaken.

According to the British, every local election in India must guarantee Muslim rights. Therefore, they held out for a system of separate electorates, whereby Muslims voted for Muslim candidates, while Hindus chose candidates from separate slates. In the eyes of Nehru and other Hindu leaders, this notion of separate representation was a sort of smokescreen masking the British aim of increasing, rather than minimizing, religious differences in India. If the British made it impossible for the two major religious groups to get along together, wouldn't they have a good excuse for postponing their departure indefinitely?

Gandhi was too gentle to make such an accusation himself. But even his patience had limits and, after weeks of useless talking about many other points that seemed minor to him, he finally spoke up quite sharply.

"This is my position, then," he said. "You cannot expect me to fill in all the details and tell you what I mean by control over the Army, finance and economic policies. We have to know first what the British government is prepared to offer India. Then, if it is acceptable, we can easily fill in the details."

Nobody was surprised when the round table conference ended early in December without really accomplishing anything.

·9·
"Quit India!"

Gandhi arrived back in Bombay on December 28, 1931, and just one week later he was thrown into jail again.

This time the imprisonment had more to do with events in England than in India itself. Under the economic stresses caused by the great worldwide Depression that had started in America in 1929, there had been a British political upheaval—bringing to power several Cabinet ministers who strongly opposed any further negotiations about Indian freedom.

As a result, riots flared up in some areas of India. The British government countered with strict new emergency rules that the Congress party condemned. Suddenly, dozens of its leaders, including Nehru and then Gandhi himself, were all behind bars.

As in the past, Gandhi used his enforced leisure to study religious writings and do some writing himself. But, briefly, near the beginning of his prison stay, he made headlines again, by embarking on a "fast unto death."

He announced this awesome penance in response to a British plan involving India's approximately fifty million untouchables. While Gandhi called them *Harijans*, to the British they were "the depressed class." As a means of giving this lowly minority representation in local law-making bodies, the British proposed making it a separate electorate with its own separate list of candidates in provincial elections.

Despite Gandhi's fervent efforts to help the *Harijans* himself, he was horrified by the British scheme, seeing it as a sure way of making untouchability even more of a permanent fact of Indian life than it was already. Instead of legitimizing this lowly condition, he wanted to end it.

He felt so deeply about this issue that he decided he must take a drastic step. Although on every previous fast he had drunk a small glass of water every hour, now he made up his mind that, besides denying himself any food, he would not have a single drop of liquid either. This vow created a full-scale crisis.

Gandhi tried to make it clear that he was not fasting against the British, but rather to reach the hearts of the tens of millions of his fellow Hindus who continued to abide by their religion's rigid code of rules, making degraded outcasts of the poor souls born into *Harijan* families. In ancient times, this group had been subjugated and forced to work at only the most menial tasks like sweeping the streets. Because of the Hindu doctrine that obedience to caste rules would be rewarded after death with a higher status in another incarnation, this form of virtual slavery had lasted for hundreds of years.

Almost overnight, Gandhi's dangerous fast

brought a swift wave of reform. Because he was sixty-two years old and under extreme emotional stress, everybody understood that he might not survive more than a few days. All over India, orthodox Hindus hurriedly examined their own consciences.

Then, in city after city, the doors of Hindu temples were flung open to *Harijan* worshipers, who had never before been allowed to enter any holy place. Leading Hindu businessmen arranged public dinners where Indians of every caste ate together as brothers. Telegrams telling of such actions were delivered to Gandhi's prison yard, where they made a stack more than six feet high.

Meanwhile, a complicated series of compromises concerning details of the British electoral plan was being worked out via cabled messages between New Delhi and London. The British certainly did not want Gandhi to die now. If that were to happen, they feared it would be impossible to prevent terrible bloodshed, as his anguished supporters struck out against those in charge of maintaining law and order.

On the sixth day of this epic fast, when Gandhi was so weak he could hardly move his head, the provisions of a much less objectionable election system were read aloud to him as he lay motionless on his cot. Would he accept this? "Excellent," he whispered.

Amid the huge surge of relief found around the country following word that the Mahatma had taken a glass of orange juice, one voice—loving but sarcastic—spoke to him privately. From another jail where she had been detained with women prisoners, Kasturbai was brought to his bedside. Shaking her head over his feeble appearance, she chided him: "Again the same story, eh?"

Gandhi smiled. Nobody else ever talked to him sharply, the way his wife of nearly fifty years did, but he still liked having her near him. Despite her bewilderment at some of his ideas, she had always been a good wife to him, much better than he deserved.

Gandhi could not help sighing occasionally over his failure as a parent. He loved little children, any children. Yet he had undoubtedly been too absorbed with his own concerns to give his four sons the personal attention they should have had during their growing-up years. Also, perhaps he had expected too much of them.

Now his eldest, Harilal, was a very sad case. He had left the ashram, become a Muslim, and turned into a homeless drunkard. Manilal had left the ashram, too, but he was doing good among the Indians back in South Africa. Ramdas was managing a small business in a distant corner of India. Only Devadas, the youngest, had stayed close, and he served as his father's secretary.

Gandhi did not often brood about his private woes. Once a friend had asked him, "How is your family?" Without hesitating, the Mahatma replied, "All of India is my family."

After recovering quite rapidly from his severe fast, Gandhi soon resumed his usual prison routine of reading and writing. When he was finally released, near the end of 1933, he began another tour of India's villages, seeking to assure himself that the treatment of *Harijans* actually had improved.

Mahatma Gandhi with Jawaharlal Nehru, India's first Prime Minister after independence.

Mahatma Gandhi

While what he saw did not satisfy him, the new attitude fostered by his fast had surely wrought some changes. Gandhi spent the next few years pressing for further steps toward full equality. He also continued to promote his other basic ideas about spinning, better health habits, and a higher standard of education.

He left politics mostly to Nehru. A fine-looking man, a compelling speaker, and a marvel at organizing, Nehru would win the world's respect as the first ruler of an independent India, Gandhi had decided. Twenty years younger than Gandhi, he and the Mahatma had a close and loving relationship.

But Gandhi's detachment from day-to-day involvement in the continuing struggle for independence abruptly ended in 1939 with the outbreak of World War II. Urgent questions arose then about how much help Indians could or should give Britain in its desperate fight against Nazi Germany and, later on, Japan. "I do not want England to be defeated or humiliated," Gandhi kept insisting. Yet he had come to feel strongly that the price of India's support of the war effort must be an immediate, definite promise of Indian independence.

By 1942, new negotiations toward this end had all but collapsed, and Gandhi began thinking about another campaign of civil disobedience using the slogan, "Quit India!"

It was Winston Churchill who, in effect, gave the signal for the new drive. At the beginning of the war, when Britain's very survival had been in doubt, this marvelously courageous man had become his country's prime minister. He was a mag-

"Quit India!"

nificent leader in most respects, but he retained a closed mind on the subject of India.

In London, in the autumn of 1942, Churchill pronounced unyieldingly: "I have not become the King's First Minister in order to preside at the liquidation of the British Empire."

Then, all over India fresh posters were slapped onto walls, and their message was direct. Everywhere, the same words were continually chalked or chanted: *"Quit India!"*

Even as British officials in India went through the motions of trying to suppress the protests, it was clear to almost everybody that independence would have to be granted soon. After all, Britain and her allies were engaged in the greatest armed conflict the world had ever seen—defending freedom. How, then, could Britain continue to keep more than four hundred million Indians from gaining control over their own destiny?

But Churchill remained adamant. Once more, Gandhi was placed behind bars. As soon as this news was published, India erupted in virtual revolt, with mobs burning British police buildings, pulling up railroad tracks, even beating and killing some British residents. The bloody rioting distressed the Mahatma so intensely that, even though he was past the age of seventy, he fasted for three weeks until the violence ceased. Upon surviving this penance, he then had to bear the personal sorrow of the death of his wife.

Early in May of 1944, Gandhi finally was released from what would prove to be the last of his many jail terms. By now, the tide had turned in the war, and it appeared to be only a matter of time until the

Allied cause triumphed. Events began to move rapidly.

Anticipating that independence was about to become a reality at last, Gandhi spent the next year trying to solve a major problem created—it seemed to him—by the wrong-headed stubbornness of another political figure. Mohammed Ali Jinnah, the most prominent leader of India's Muslims, had originally entered politics as a firm ally of the Mahatma in the All-India Congress. But over the years Jinnah had changed.

Jinnah was a tall, thin man with a large ego. Some of the Mahatma's associates thought it was personal jealousy that had made Jinnah stop cooperating with Gandhi. Others attributed the break to British influence. Whatever the reason, Jinnah had formed his own competing organization called the Muslim League. Now he appeared bent on dividing India irrevocably.

As independence approached, he kept insisting that India's Muslims would not be satisfied by anything less than a separate state of their own, to be called Pakistan. The fact that the majority of the country's Muslims—about one-quarter of India's total population—lived in two separate areas, one in the east and the other in the west, with a big chunk of predominantly Hindu territory between them, did not strike Jinnah as an impediment. He did not even want to discuss details like Pakistan's borders with Gandhi. He simply stated that he would settle such matters with the British at the appropriate time.

Gandhi pleaded in every way he could think of to make Jinnah modify his stand. He wrote imploring

"Quit India!"

letters about the urgency of unifying, rather than dividing, India, addressing his appeals to "Dear Brother Jinnah." Jinnah's replies were addressed coldly to "Mr. Gandhi."

This difficult problem was consuming Gandhi's mind to the exclusion of almost everything else when, in May of 1945, stirring news flashed around the world. Germany had surrendered! Only two months later, although the Japanese still remained to be beaten, there was a national election in Great Britain. Winston Churchill's Conservative party suffered a stunning defeat.

Gandhi with Jinnah, who became the first Prime Minister of Pakistan.

Mahatma Gandhi

It was as if the British realized, with the war nearly won, that another sort of leadership would be needed to direct their country's course in a world at peace.

The new government of Britain was headed by Clement R. Atlee, the leader of the Labour party. One of his first official acts was to issue a statement favoring "an early realization of self-government in India."

10

A Tragic Victory

*I*t took two more years to work out the necessary arrangements for the British departure from India. This was the most frustrating period of Gandhi's long life, as he himself admitted. From 1915 through 1947, his main object had been securing his country's freedom. Finally, when the goal was in sight, he sadly declared that thirty-two years of striving "have come to an inglorious end."

For, instead of the united, independent India that Gandhi had envisioned, the country was going to be partitioned in a way that he believed would inevitably cause terrible trouble. Because the stern Jinnah had insisted so rigidly on the separate Muslim state of Pakistan, everybody else involved in the negotiations reluctantly accepted his plan.

Then, even before the momentous ceremony of lowering the British flag in the capital city of New Delhi took place, the Mahatma's worst fears began to come true. Bloody fighting between Hindus and Muslims broke out in Calcutta.

Independence Day was August 15, 1947, but Gandhi refused to take part in any celebration. He did not even issue a statement commemorating the occasion. He spent the day alone, fasting and praying.

Mahatma Gandhi

Soon Gandhi would reach the age of seventy-eight. In happier moments, he had joked about being such a tough bird that he would surely live to be a hundred and twenty-five. Despite all his fasting, only his face had become gaunt and wrinkled; the rest of his body remained smoothly wiry from his habit of striding great distances almost every day. Over the next few weeks, however, he turned into a feeble-looking old man.

This was because the frenzy of killing, which he had tried so hard to avert, was spreading throughout the land. Indians were brutally murdering other Indians in their fury about the way some major provinces had been carved up as part of the partition plan.

To Gandhi the horror was particularly searing. He felt sure it could have been avoided, if only he had been wise enough to find the path to Jinnah's heart. In tens of thousands of Indian villages, Hindus and Muslims had been living side by side for many generations, mostly peacefully. Only comparatively recently, in crowded cities, had serious religious strife erupted. Even so, the Mahatma had believed his own teachings were gradually bringing about a more brotherly relationship.

But Jinnah would not agree. His supporters were mainly prosperous Muslim businessmen who hoped to become the ruling class in the new Pakistan, rather than just a minority among the more numerous ranks of well-educated Hindus. Also, Jinnah himself obviously wished to preside in Pakistan, finally achieving the international recognition he thought he deserved.

At the last minute, just before the adoption of the partition plan, Gandhi had gone so far as to offer

A Tragic Victory

Jinnah the post of prime minister in the new, united India. Nehru, not too happily, agreed to take this risk and step aside himself. Nevertheless, Jinnah suspected some sort of trickery and refused the offer.

The stage was set for an awful spectacle. Beyond the rioting in many cities, there was something else the world had never witnessed—*two* enormous streams of refugees, uprooted from their homes by terror and the fear of what might happen to them and their families if they remained where they were. Hindus fled in one direction, Muslims in the other. Altogether, an estimated fifteen million men, women, and children took part in the mass exodus.

Since these pitiful processions were traveling on parallel paths, clashes often occurred. Many people lacked food and water. There were no facilities for them when they reached wherever they thought they would be safe, and many diseases flourished in the emergency camps.

Mahatma Gandhi continued to preach love and peace. At the height of all this upheaval, he was heard by one of his aides murmuring to himself: "What shall I do? What shall I do?"

At the beginning of September, reports about the strife in Calcutta became so alarming that Gandhi took the only step he could. Weak as he was, he proclaimed that until the violence there ended, he would once more "fast unto death."

Scores of anxious visitors descended on the Delhi house where the Mahatma was staying. All sorts of pledges were made, and his penance appeared to bring peace, at least, to Calcutta. After three days, Gandhi relented, to the relief of all.

Nevertheless, it was beyond even the Mahatma

to stop the frightful bloodshed along the frontiers between India and Pakistan. Despite his increasing frailty, he insisted on traveling to some of the worst areas, often on foot and accompanied only by a few of his loyal disciples. He could no longer convince himself that he was accomplishing much. Yet, as long as he lived, he could not stop trying.

By January of 1948, Gandhi was staying at the home of a well-off supporter on the outskirts of Delhi. It was too dangerous, even in the capital, for him to follow his usual practice of camping among the poorest inhabitants of any place he visited. Some of his close associates, including Prime Minister Nehru, urged him to have guards with him whenever he ventured out, but the Mahatma brushed aside these worries about his personal safety.

He conducted prayers every evening in the large open space adjoining the house where he was staying. Anyone was welcome at these sessions—Hindu, Muslim, Sikh, or Christian—it did not matter to Gandhi. But since the conflict between Muslims and Hindus had created so much turmoil, he made a point of having at each of his public prayer sessions some passages read from the Koran, the sacred book of the Muslims.

Around 4:30 P.M on January 30, 1948, the Mahatma had his usual supper of cooked and raw vegetables and some goat's milk. At 5:00, he smiled and said, "I must tear myself away." About five hundred people had gathered to await his appearance at evening prayers, and he could not disappoint them.

Often when Gandhi arrived in front of a large

A Tragic Victory

crowd, he did not address them with any words. Touching his palms together in the traditional Hindu greeting, he would squat on the wooden platform from which he overlooked the gathering and simply sway from side to side. Without any signal, the crowd facing him would sway in unison. It was a remarkable, wordless communication.

On this evening, Gandhi had time only to smile, touch his palms together, and extend an unspoken blessing. Then, in the front row of the crowd, only a few feet from the Mahatma, a young man reached into his pocket and drew out a pistol.

Three shots were fired.

The smile faded from Gandhi's face. "Oh, God!" he murmured. Then he fell over, dead.

Throughout India, the shock was beyond measure. Within only a few seconds, the assailant had been captured. Thankfully, he proved to be a Hindu—a young Hindu who belonged to an extremist group convinced it was the Mahatma's fault that Pakistan had been allowed to come into existence.

Had the murderer been a Muslim, there is no telling what horror might have resulted from a blazing spirit of revenge among the Hindu majority. As it was, the entire country mourned Gandhi without any further violence.

In keeping with Hindu practice, a pile of logs was assembled beside a holy river. A huge throng stood watching in almost total silence as Gandhi's son, Ramdas, lit the funeral pyre. The body of the Mahatma lay above the logs with his head to the north, as is prescribed in holy writings.

When the flames leapt upward, engulfing the

Mahatma Gandhi

remains of Gandhi, awesome wails burst from the horde of mourners. Then came silence again. At dusk, a boat slowly moved toward the middle of the

The body of Mahatma Gandhi lying in state in Birla House, New Delhi on January 31, 1948.

A Tragic Victory

river, and Ramdas scattered the ashes of his saintly father over the water.

From every part of the world, tributes to Mahatma Gandhi went far beyond the usual words used in mourning even an outstanding statesman or spiritual leader. Perhaps the most moving words of all were spoken by another of the towering figures

Mahatma Gandhi

of the twentieth century. Albert Einstein, who had himself added immensely to humanity's store of knowledge about physical science, said of Gandhi:

"Generations to come, it may be, will scarce believe that such a one as this ever in flesh and blood walked upon this earth."

Postscript

The Indian poet Tagore once said of Gandhi:

> Perhaps he will not succeed. Perhaps he will fail as Christ failed to wean men from their iniquities, but he will always be remembered as one who made his life a lesson for all ages to come.

In the nearly four decades since Gandhi's death, these words have come to seem increasingly perceptive. Perhaps in some ways, Gandhi *did* fail. Surely, much that has happened on the Indian subcontinent during the years after the departure of the British would have deeply disappointed him.

Despite many notable steps toward democracy, and toward raising the vast Indian population out of its awful poverty, the coming of independence by no means brought lasting peace. A series of border disputes between India and Pakistan led to a brief war in 1971, as a result of which part of Pakistan broke away and formed another separate state called Bangladesh. Periodically, tensions involving these neighboring lands remind the rest of the world that Gandhi's dream of brotherhood throughout the whole area has not yet been realized.

Even within India itself, political stability and tranquillity have not always prevailed. After Prime Minister Nehru died in 1968, there were serious threats of factional dispute. His daughter Indira—who had married a man named Gandhi, but who was not related to the Mahatma—was chosen as her father's successor. While Indira Gandhi proved a

Mahatma Gandhi

strong, unifying force, her leadership over the years became too much like that of a dictator for the friends of Indian democracy to feel comfortable with her at the helm.

Then she, too, was assassinated. In 1984, a conspiracy among her own guards brought her death—and a new wave of religious rioting broke out, this time between the Sikhs and the Hindus. Her son Rajiv was chosen to take over as prime minister. Whether Rajiv Gandhi will be able to rule the country successfully is a question only the passage of time can answer.

Through all of these difficulties, though, the fame of Mahatma Gandhi has continued to grow. The period following India's independence was marked by similar anti-colonial struggles in Africa and elsewhere in Asia, and Gandhi's policies inspired the freedom forces in many lands. He also had a great effect on the civil rights movement that began stirring new hope among black Americans during the 1950s.

Martin Luther King, Jr., the outstanding leader of this drive, often spoke of Mahatma Gandhi's influence on his own thinking. It was Gandhi who taught King the lesson of nonviolent protest, and King's debt to Gandhi is testified to by a long shelf of books at the research center built in King's memory in Atlanta, Georgia.

Thousands of miles from India, eighty volumes containing Gandhi's writings are on display, because the words of the Mahatma had such a profound impact on a young black American when he was studying for the ministry.

Postscript

Ved Mehta, a noted Indian writer, most aptly summed up Gandhi's continuing importance:

> His ideas have application wherever there are poor, oppressed people—even in the richest country in the world.

A Note on Sources

It is rare for the writers of a factual biography to use a motion picture in their research. But Sir Richard Attenborough's award winning 1982 film *Gandhi* was itself the product of painstaking research carried out during a twenty-year period. It provides an awesome, panoramic view of the Mahatma's career. Any reader who would like to *see* a portrayal of such events as the Salt March should do as the authors of this book started out by doing and take advantage of the videocassette recorder to watch the gifted actor Ben Kingsley's portrayal of Gandhi.

But helpful as the film is visually, it must be remembered that it is not really a historical record. For dramatic purposes, a certain amount of conversation had to be invented and sometimes other minor additions or subtractions mar the accuracy of the screenplay.

Thus, this biography of Gandhi is fundamentally based on more traditional source material, mainly Gandhi's own autobiography. The edition most readily available is the paperback, *An Autobiography: The Story of My Experiments With Truth* by Mohandas K. Gandhi, translated from the original in Gujarati by Mahadev Desai, published by Beacon Press of Boston in 1957.

Suggested Further Readings

Alexander, Horace. *Gandhi Through Western Eyes*. New York: Asia Publishing House, 1969.

Fisher, Louis. *Gandhi: His Life and Message for the World*. New York: New American Library, 1954.

———. *The Life of Mahatma Gandhi*. New York: Harper and Brothers, 1950.

Gold, Gerald. *Gandhi: A Pictorial Biography*. New York: Newmarket Press, 1963.

Mehta, Ved. *Mahatma Gandhi and His Apostles*. New York: Viking Press, 1977.

Rolland, Romain. *Mahatma Gandhi*. New York: Century Company, 1924.

Sheean, Vincent. *Mahatma Gandhi: A Great Life in Brief*. New York: Knopf, 1955.

Shirer, William L. *Gandhi*. New York: Simon & Schuster, 1979.

Index

Ahmedabad ashram, 64-65
All-India Congress, 78-79, 88
Amritsar massacre, 69-70
Atlee, Clement R., 102

Bangladesh, 111
Bhagavad Gita, 36-37
British East India Company, 12
British salt laws, 80-85

Caste system, 15, 50, 94
Christianity, Gandhi and, 38, 50
Churchill, Winston, 86-88, 98-99, 101
"Civil Disobedience" (essay), 74
"Coolies," 42

Dandi (town), 81
Durban (port), 42
Dyer, General Reginald, 70

Einstein, Albert, quoted on Gandhi, 110

Fasting: as Hindu custom, 13-14; Gandhi and, 56
Fasts: first public fast, 66; for rights of untouchables, 93-95; in home of Muslim, 76-77
Fingerprinting law, 52-54

Gandhi (film), 115
Gandhi, Devadas (son), 96
Gandhi, Harilal (son), 39-40, 96
Gandhi, Indira, 111-12
Gandhi, Karamchand (Kaba) (father), 14-15, 16-17, 26-27
Gandhi, Kasturbai (wife), 16, 18, 30, 39, 55-56, 95-96
Gandhi, Laxmidas (brother), 24

Index

Gandhi, Mahatma:
All-India Congress and, 78-79; and the play, *Harischandra*, 19-20; arrests, 53, 93, 99; as candidate for the bar, 33-34, 38; as husband and father, 39-40, 55-56, 96; assassination of, 107; at Round Table Conference (1931), 88-92; at school, 13; at talks in New Delhi (1931), 86-88; autobiography of, 7, 74; begins to simplify his life, 51-52; birthplace, 11; college education, 28-29; conceives philosophy of *Satyagraha* (Soul Force), 53; concern over British rule in India, 20-21; concern with morality, 19; continues quest for religion, 50-51; devotes himself to Indian struggle in South Africa, 45-46; eating of meat and, 21-24, 31, 34-35; establishes ashram near Ahmedabad, 64-65; experiences prejudice in Durban, 42-44; fast in home of Muslim, 76-77; fast to protest British plan for untouchables, 93-95; fast to protest partitioning of India, 105; fasting and, 56; father's death and, 26-28; first public fast, 66; full name, 7, 11; funeral of, 107-09; gives new name to untouchables, 77; in high school, 19; is admitted to British bar, 38; Mohammed Ali Jinnah and, 100-01; joins Vegetarian Society, 34-35; law practice in South Africa, 47-50; leads textile workers' strike, 65-66; leaves for South Africa, 42; marriage of, 15-17; meaning of *Gandhi*, 15; meeting with Tagore, 61; mother's influence, 13-14; nationwide *hartal* (1919), 68-70; origin of *Mahatma*, 7, 61-62; personal characteristics, 7; physical characteristics, 13; protest against fingerprinting law, 52-54; protest against Smuts' punitive laws, 58-59; reads *Bhagavad Gita*, 36-37; return to India (1891), 39; return to India (1915), 61; revives rural spinning, 76; salt laws protests (1930), 80-81; sets sail for England (1888), 30-31; sets up cooperative farm near

Index

Durban (1910), 57-58; smoking and, 24; social class, 15; studies in London, 33; travels to Pretoria, 44-45; trial and imprisonment (1922), 71-75; visits British mill workers, 89-90; Western culture and, 32; writings of Jesus and, 38;
Gandhi, Manilal (son), 96
Gandhi, Putlibai (mother), 13-14, 39
Gandhi, Rajiv, 112
Gandhi, Ramdas (son), 96, 107, 109
Gokhale, Gopal K., 58, 63-64

Harijans, 77
Harischandra (play), 19-20
Hartal (1919), 68-70
Hindu-Muslim conflict, 67; establishment of state of Pakistan and, 103-05; Gandhi's response (1924), 76-77; Round Table Conference and, 91-92
Hindus and Hinduism: *Bhagavad Gita*, 36-37; caste system, 15, 50, 94; early marriage, 15-17, 18; fasting, 13-14; food reform movement, 22; funeral rites, 107-09; incarnation, 15; meat-eating, 21-22; wedding celebration, 17

Incarnation, 15
India: Amritsar massacre, 69-70; British salt laws protests (1930), 80-85; caste system, 15, 50, 94; during World War II, 98-99; early history, 12; Indira Gandhi and, 111-12; Independence Day, 103; Muslim League, 100; nationwide *hartal* (1919), 68-70; partitioning of, 103-05; political restrictions after the war (1918), 67-68; protests for rights of untouchables (1932), 93-95; revival of spinning, 76; Round Table Conference (1931), 88-92; status under British rule, 20; war with Pakistan (1971), 111
Indigo sharecroppers, 67
Inner Temple, 33

Jesus Christ, writings of, 38
Jinnah, Mohammed Ali, 100-01, 104-05
Joshiji, 28-29

King, Martin Luther, Jr., Gandhi's influence, 112

121

Index

Koran (holy book), 50
Krishna, 37

Lathi, 82, 85
"Lead, Kindly Light" (hymn), 50
London University, 33

Mahatma (title), 7, 61
Meat-eating, 21-24, 31, 34-35
Mehta, Ved, 113
Mehtab (friend), 21-24
Miller, Webb, 85
Muslim League, 100
Muslims and Muslim customs: eating of meat, 22; fingerprinting law and, 54; the Koran, 50; 1906 desire for separate state, 100

Nehru, Jawaharlal, 88, 93, 98, 111
New Delhi, talks at (1931), 86-88
Nonviolent protest, 52-53

Pakistan, 100, 103-05, 111
Parsees, 67
Partition, of India, 103-05
Passive resistance, 53

Peaceful disobedience, 52
Porbandar (town), 11, 13
Pretoria (city), 44

Round Table Conference (1931), 88-92

Salt laws protests, 80-85
Salt March (1930), 80-81
Satyagraha, 53, 66
Sikhs, 67
Smoking, Gandhi and, 24
Smuts, Jan Christian, 53-54, 58-59
Song Celestial, The, 36-37
Soul Force, 53, 66
South Africa, 42-46, 49, 52-54, 58-59
Spinning, revival of, 76

Tagore, Rabindranath, 61, 79, 111
Textile workers' strike (Ahmedabad), 65-66
Thoreau, Henry David, 74
Untouchables, 15, 50, 77, 93-95

Vegetarian Society, 34-35

World War I, 63
World War II, 98-102

About the Authors

Doris and Harold Faber have written numerous biographies, together and separately. They both began their careers as reporters for *The New York Times*, which Harold continues to represent as its Hudson Valley correspondent. They have two grown daughters, and they live on a farm in upstate New York where they grow a lot of vegetables while pursuing their literary activities.